Weird War One

Dedication
To my parents, who taught me to love
the strange and the silly

Weird War One

Intriguing Items and Fascinating Feats
from the First World War

Peter Taylor with Philip Dutton

Published by IWM,
Lambeth Road, London SE1 6HZ
iwm.org.uk

© The Trustees of the Imperial War Museum, 2015.

ISBN 978-1-904897-84-2

A catalogue record for this book is available from the British Library.
Printed in Italy by Printer Trento.

Every effort has been made to contact all copyright holders. The publishers will be glad to make good in future editions any error or omissions brought to their attention.

10 9 8 7 6 5 4 3 2 1

Front cover image: A Lieutenant (left) and NCO (right) serving with the Imperial German Army. Their unusual headgear was most likely to have helped pinpoint the position of enemy guns, possibly by enhancing the booms and flashes. Image courtesy Drake Goodman © Artist's Estate.

Back cover image: A soldier sits inside a fake 'observation tree' made of canvas and steel, near Souchez, May 1918. © IWM (Q10308).

Design by Carole Ash and Philip Gilderdale at Project 360.

Contents

Introduction

THE DISPLAYS, ARCHIVES and store rooms of Imperial War Museums offer plenty of evidence of the 'horrid, ghastly thing' that was the First World War. But if you're looking for the horrors of war, you won't find them here. This book doesn't pretend to be a serious, weighty history of the Great War. Rather, it's a catalogue of the weird, the wonderful and the downright eccentric, from deep within the archives.

Did you know that pigeons parachuted? That it took more than a quarter of a million cows to make a Zeppelin? That the tank was known as a wibble-wobble? That thousands of children collected conkers to be used for munitions?

MOP FIGHTING

Mounted on each others backs, soldiers engage in an exciting mop fight. One of the items at the Military sports at Felixstowe.

Weird War One offers you a glimpse of these and many other First World War phenomena. Flick through the pages and you'll find a most eclectic collection of images, covering everything from dazzling camouflage to shovel shields, trench gardening to mop fighting, invisible ink to kaiser toilet roll. You'll read the stories of all kinds of forgotten people, like Boy Scout defenders, death-defying servicemen, brilliant inventors and hapless spies. And you'll come away with so many bizarre and interesting facts that you'll enjoy asking people, 'Did you know...?'

This book tells a story of the 'war to end all wars' that's often untold. Quite rightly, the First World War is remembered as colossally and terribly destructive. But amid all that darkness, there was light: creativity and innovation, ingenuity and courage, camaraderie and humour. It is that amazing spirit, expressed in so many ways by so many people, that this book aims to celebrate.

Leaders

FROM SNOW SCULPTURES
TO TOBY JUGS

PAGE 8
Snow sculpture allegedly portraying the kaiser, made by loyal Germans on the Western Front, Reims, 1915. Not a bad likeness, although the revered emperor has the arm span of a tyrannosaurus-rex.

PAGE 9
This Toby jug depicts **Marshal Ferdinand Foch** on the champers, which is inscribed *au diable le kaiser* (devil take the kaiser). Foch became commander-in-chief of the Allied Forces on the Western Front during the crisis of the German offensives in late spring 1918.

WINSTON CHURCHILL said of the wise and cautious commander-in-chief of the Royal Navy, Sir John Jellicoe, that he was 'the only man who could lose the war in an afternoon'. This observation starkly illuminates the terrible responsibilities of those in positions of power during wartime. With the stakes so high, enormous power was invested in men with clout, vision and a rigid backbone.

The military and political leaders were the celebrities of their time, and you couldn't go anywhere without seeing their faces – on newspaper front pages, on posters, on statues. They became the focus for spectacular displays of patriotism. People dedicated songs and artworks to their icons. They wrote stories for them and about them, and sent letters conveying their admiration (and, occasionally, romantic intentions!).

And they bought merchandise, all manner of merchandise. Want to show your support for Hindenburg? Use a matchbox engraved with his likeness. Think Kitchener's got style? Wash with his soap. Idolise Wilson? Pop a Woodrow Toby jug on your shelf.

All of this adulation was excellent for fostering unity and positivity. But it placed enormous burdens on the leaders to deliver what was expected of them. This war of unprecedented scale and complexity produced unique problems. Inevitably, the war took its toll, and some leaders gave up the ghost or were shunted out. But for every leader who fell, another was lined up to take his place, with energy, optimism and, sometimes, talent.

Adolf Hitler in the jubilant crowd which gathered to celebrate the declaration of war on the Odeon Platz in Munich,1914. This remarkable photo was taken by Heinrich Hoffmann, who later became Hitler's official photographer.

On the 20th anniversary of the war's outbreak, the photograph was widely published in the press — but only after Hitler had seen to it that his original luxuriant moustache was doctored to resemble the famous 'toothbrush'. Adolf Hitler: a pioneer of retouching.

Lord Kitchener
as featured on this
recruitment poster

A CRASH COURSE ON LEADING PERSONALITIES

Lord Kitchener took up the post of secretary of state for war in August 1914 with widespread approval. A solid and imperturbable soldier, he realised early on that the war would be a long one and he set in motion the raising of a mass army. The setbacks of 1915 lowered his prestige, and he was gradually sidelined by the Asquith government. Nonetheless, his heroic appeal was so powerful that following his death at sea in June 1916, some people refused to accept his loss, preferring to regard him, like some long-lost Arthurian figure, as merely sleeping and secretly waiting for the day he would return and save his country.

Winston Churchill's career in the First World War blurred the roles of politician and soldier. In October 1911 he was made first lord of the admiralty, but was later blamed for the Navy's failure to secure the Dardanelles (a key reason for the failure of the Gallipoli campaign), and was demoted in the Cabinet in May 1915. After resigning from the government in November 1915, he dived into 'service under fire' on the Western Front with the Royal Scots Fusiliers, before returning to politics in June 1916.

David Lloyd George had charisma, charm and eloquence by the bucket load, which saw him rise up the ranks. Chancellor of the Exchequer at the war's outbreak, he was made minister of munitions in May 1915 and facilitated a hugely improved armaments production. In June 1916 he became secretary of state for war, and then he moved to Number 10 Downing Street in December of that year. As Prime Minister, Lloyd George took an active role in strategy and repeatedly clashed with military

David Lloyd George

Kaiser Wilhelm II

and naval leaders. His dynamism, his effect on morale and his performance as a war leader laid inspiring foundations for Churchill's leadership in the Second World War.

Woodrow Wilson, the US president, was personally appalled by the evil of war and his faith in international justice meant he committed to being a mediator only. But German unrestricted submarine warfare drew the USA into the conflict on the Allied side in April 1917, and Wilson proved a forceful wartime leader.

Kaiser Wilhelm II had always been impressed by the pomp of military heraldry. But his theatrical posturing as 'supreme warlord' served only to disguise his unpredictability and ineffectiveness as a war leader. He became a figure of fun for Allied satirists and caricaturists.

Paul von Hindenburg was recalled from retirement on the outbreak of war to work alongside **General Erich Ludendorff.** They inflicted crushing defeats on the Russians in 1914 and 1915, took command of German land forces in 1916, and dominated German domestic politics for the last two years of the war. But it was Hindenburg who was most idolised by the people, and he featured in many poster campaigns.

The British were not impressed by frowning von Hindenburg. Here he is in the form of a **wooden figure**, with an affliction the British apparently *would* wish on their worst enemy: gout.

Little Willie: Crown Prince Friedrich Wilhelm of Germany, son of Kaiser Wilhelm II and heir to the German imperial throne. This **wooden caricature figure** was made at the Lord Roberts Memorial Workshops for Disabled Soldiers and Sailors in London during the war and subsequently sold for charity.

A serious souvenir for a serious man: a silver-plated **matchbox cover** embossed with a portrait of Paul von Hindenburg. The inscription translates as 'General Field Marshal von Hindenburg, the liberator of East Prussia, 1914'.

A tin **matchbox holder** with Kaiser Wilhelm on the front and von Hindenburg on the back. The historic German motto on the side, *Viel feind, viel ehr*, means 'Many foes, much honour'.

Gun trumps nutcracker! A British **propaganda jug** from early in the war that celebrates the resistance of the British Expeditionary Force to the invading German Army in Belgium. The kaiser allegedly called the BEF a 'contemptible little army'.

In Germany, the military leader Paul von Hindenburg was the man to admire. In homage to him, colossal **wooden statues** sprang up around the country. The public donated to war charities for the honour of hammering a nail into a statue. British papers of the time pointed out that banging nails into a statue of your leader was a rather odd way of expressing your support for him.

BRITONS

"WANTS" YOU

JOIN YOUR COUNTRY'S ARMY!

GOD SAVE THE KING

Reproduced by permission of LONDON OPINION

Printed by the Victoria House Printing Co., Ltd., Tudor Street, London, E.C.

Lord Kitchener is best known these days from this much-imitated **recruitment poster**, but at the time a host of other merchandise fed the public's Kitchener-mania. You could light Kitchener matches, save in a Kitchener piggy bank, snack from a Kitchener biscuit tin and... yes, wash in **Kitchener soap**.

How do you honour
a stern, serious man?
Dedicate a jolly **song** for
him in a *Merry Moments*
musical revue.

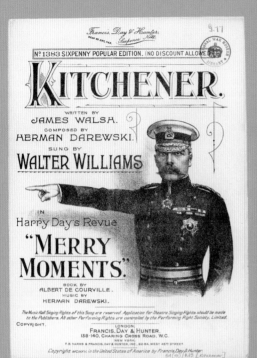

Kitchener even had his
own **doll** (or should
that be 'action figure'?).
A pretty good likeness, but
for the joint-defying feet.

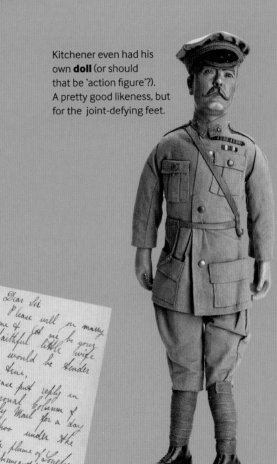

Here, one woman has been
moved to **propose** to
Kitchener, offering to become
his 'faithful little wife' who'll
be 'very quiet and no trouble
to you'. She suggests he reply
via the *Daily Mail* personal
column under the *nom de
plume* of 'Lonely'.

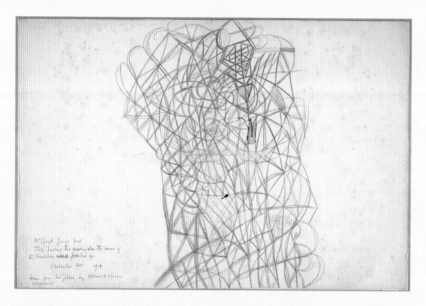

▶ American President **Woodrow Wilson's portrait** created by 21,000 US troops. Photographers Arthur Mole and John Thomas were commissioned by the US government to scale high viewing platforms and take a series of these 'living photographs' at military camps. They were meant to boost morale, and they certainly gave men great claims to fame, along the lines of, 'I was once the left nostril of our nation's president...'

A **doodle** British Prime Minister Lloyd George made on his blotter at a meeting in Versailles to discuss the terms of the Armistice, before it went into effect on 11 November 1918. The scope for interpretation is endless — a new Tower of Babel based on the metal superstructure of a crashed Zeppelin? A metaphor for the fate of the post-war world? A craving for spaghetti?

WEIRD WAR FACT

The acronym OMG (oh my God) was first used in September 1917 in a letter to Winston Churchill when he was minister of munitions. The sender was Admiral 'Jackie' Fisher, whose liberal use of exclamation marks also shows him to be in tune with today's teenagers.

Sincerely Yours,

Woodrow Wilson

000 OFFICERS AND MEN
MP SHERMAN, CHILLICOTHE, OHIO
G GEN. MATHEW C. SMITH, COMMANDING

INTERNATIONAL
COPYRIGHT

The famous political cartoonist Sir Francis Carruthers Gould designed a series of 11 **Toby jugs** based on leading Allied soldiers, sailors and statesmen that were sold between 1915 and 1919. Here, in true Toby tradition, **Kitchener** holds on his lap a jug of ale, aptly labelled 'Bitter for the Kaiser'.

Field Marshal Sir Douglas Haig sits on a British Mark 1 tank and holds (the fate of) Britain in his hands. The plinth is marked 'push and go', a reference to the so-called Big Push: the Battle of the Somme in which Haig was sure the tank would prove itself to be the new wonder weapon. Sadly this wasn't to be the case, and the tank only came into its own later.

'He's got the whole world in his hands...' Quite a responsibility for **King George V**, depicted here in naval uniform and seated on an elaborate gilded throne with lion arm-rests. Beneath the inscription reads *pro patria* – for country. This level of patriotism came with a hefty price tag: seven guineas a jug, or £62 today!

Field Marshal Sir John French clasps an ale jug in the French national colours inscribed with *French pour les Francais* (French for the French). Sir John commanded the British Expeditionary Force on the Western Front from the outbreak of war until December 1915. Ironically given his name and posting, maintaining good relations with the French tested him to his limits.

David Lloyd George was in charge of gearing up war production post-June 1915. Here the 'Welsh Wizard' is supporting a large-calibre artillery shell marked 'Shell Out'.

Admiral of the Fleet Sir John Jellicoe, holding a jug inscribed with his nickname, 'Hell Fire Jack'. An original certificate issued by the London retailer Soane & Smith in 1915 records Jellicoe as 'proving the most effective antidote to "U" warfare'.

General (later Marshal) Joseph Joffre holding an artillery shell associated with the famous French 75 field gun. Joffre (nicknamed 'Papa') was commander of the French forces between 1914 and 1916.

'Welcome Uncle Sam', declares this Toby jug. **President of the USA Woodrow Wilson** is flying to Europe astride a seaplane.

Soldiering On

FROM FLY WHISKS TO THE GHOST OF ST GEORGE

PAGE 22
Do you suffer from alarm-clock rage? Then pity the occupants of the **US Naval Training Camp**, Seattle, Washington who were roused with this deafening call.

PAGE 23
Bug off! A British Army standard-issue **fly swat**. In hot summer conditions especially, swarms of flies could make life intolerable for the trench garrisons — friend and foe alike.

IN THESE, THE CENTENARY YEARS of the First World War, a recurrent theme in the many commemorations and acts of remembrance is the experiences of those at the front lines, on land, at sea and in the air. The reality of war was a long nightmare of anxiety, fear, dread and boredom. And yet, the men soldiered on.

In part, the job kept them going. Structure, routines, rules, discipline, training – dull, perhaps, but motivating, and a reason to get out of bed in the morning (if the deafening bugle call wasn't impetus enough). Keeping busy meant keeping your mind off the horrors of war.

Soldiering on required a body capable of doing so. That meant resting when possible and eating the rations on offer (often at the expense of the taste buds). It meant doing what you could for personal hygiene, from scrubbing up in a tepid, shared bath to asking your mate to pick lice off you. And it meant paying attention to safety instructions, so you didn't wander into a cloud of poison gas or offer your head to the enemy as a shooting target.

The collective spirit was a boost for many men. Chums, pals and cobbers built a solid camaraderie through socialising: music and song, a game of cards, an illicit drinking session, jesting and ribbing in colourful language.

Above all, though, for many men it was a belief in something greater that carried them through – whether religion, superstition... or the protective ghost of the dragon-slaying St George.

Journalist Arthur Machen published a short story called 'The Bowmen' in London's *Evening News* in September 1914. It told of how St George summoned up archers from the Battle of Agincourt to rescue British soldiers fighting in the Battle of Mons a month earlier. For whatever reason, many readers took the story to be true, and versions of the tale swept the nation. Machen swiftly published *The Bowmen and Other Legends of War* in order to put the record straight. The book became a bestseller, but people were unimpressed by the word 'legend' in the title. The story was true, they decided, and it spurred more reports of angels on the battlefields. Perhaps the stories were started by the military – certainly, they boosted morale. This painting, ***The Vision of St George over the Battlefield*** by John Hassall, shows two British soldiers staring out over no man's land in disbelief at a vision of St George.

ARE YOU A VICTIM TO
OPTIMISM?
—o—o—o—o—
YOU DON'T KNOW?
—o—o—o—o—
THEN ASK YOURSELF THE FOLLOWING QUESTIONS.
—o—o—o—o—

1.—DO YOU SUFFER FROM CHEERFULNESS?
2.—DO YOU WAKE UP IN A MORNING FEELING THAT ALL IS GOING WELL FOR THE ALLIES?
3.—DO YOU SOMETIMES THINK THAT THE WAR WILL END WITHIN THE NEXT TWELVE MONTHS?
4.—DO YOU BELIEVE GOOD NEWS IN PREFERENCE TO BAD?
5.—DO YOU CONSIDER OUR LEADERS ARE COMPETENT TO CONDUCT THE WAR TO A SUCCESSFUL ISSUE?

IF YOUR ANSWER IS "YES" TO ANYONE OF THESE QUESTIONS THEN YOU ARE IN THE CLUTCHES OF THAT DREAD DISEASE.

WE CAN CURE YOU.

TWO DAYS SPENT AT OUR ESTABLISHMENT WILL EFFECTUALLY ERADICATE ALL TRACES OF IT FROM YOUR SYSTEM.

DO NOT HESITATE—APPLY FOR TERMS AT ONCE TO:—

Messrs. Walthorpe, Foxley, Nelmes and Co.

TELEPHONE 72, "GRUMBLESTONES."   TELEGRAMS: "GROUSE."

STOP! & THINK!!!
—o—o—o—
Messrs. NUNTHORPE, COX & CO. Are now opening their book on the
Summer Meeting.
—o—o—o—
THE OLD LIBERAL PRICES ARE ON OFFER.
5 1 the field for the BAPAUME STAKES
All in, Run or not.
We Always Pay!!!
—o—o—o—
Midsummer Handicap.
1 3 ATKINS and ANZAC.
100 1 THE FLYING HUN.
—o—o—o—
Do not trust financial crocks,
Put it on with Nunthorpe, Cox.
—o—o—o—
Telegrams: "REDTABS."
Telephone: Six Lines, "102 Back'um."

Mr. HOWFIELD
Begs to notify his many kind Patrons that he and Mr. CAULETT have DISSOLVED PARTNERSHIP owing to a little difference of opinion and he is carrying on business in NEW and COMMODIOUS PREMISES with
Mr. NORLETT.
—o—o—o—
COME & INSPECT OUR
New styles in fine Tiles
Great cops in gorgeous props
AND REMEMBER THAT
If you're going o'er the bags,
Come and see our new glad rags.
—o—o—o—
THE SAME FINANCIAL LATITUDE ALLOWED OUR CUSTOMERS AS HITHERTO.

A **spoof advert** from the *Wipers Times* in July 1916 inspired by the disastrous Battle of the Somme. This hilarious but also grimly satirical magazine was published by front-line soldiers from 1916 until the end of the war. It was printed on a press that a captain of the 12th Battalion Sherwood Foresters had found abandoned in a cellar in Ypres. The magazine's name poked fun at soldiers' mispronunciation of 'Ypres', and its contents invariably poked fun at military leaders.

Here's a **fly whisk**, used by General Sir Ian Hamilton, commander-in-chief of the Mediterranean Expeditionary Force at Gallipoli, 1915. He wrote: 'This little fly whisk travelled all over the world with me for the four years which I was Inspector General of Overseas Forces… At the Dardanelles it was always in my hand and has been in all the trenches as well as on the *Queen Elizabeth*.' Quite possibly the most well-travelled fly swat in existence.

Look closely at this First World War soldier.

Notice anything unusual?

This isn't your average guy in uniform — in fact, it's a gal! **Dorothy Lawrence** was the only female British soldier during the First World War. After her request to work as a war correspondent was rejected, she disguised herself as a man, got some false papers and joined a British Expeditionary Force tunnelling company. After ten days of laying mines under enemy trenches, she handed herself in. The Army was highly embarrassed and made her swear to keep her story to herself. She did — until after the war, when she published an account of her adventures.

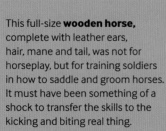

This full-size **wooden horse,** complete with leather ears, hair, mane and tail, was not for horseplay, but for training soldiers in how to saddle and groom horses. It must have been something of a shock to transfer the skills to the kicking and biting real thing.

The Kent Cyclists Battalion in 1915.

At the beginning of the war all sides believed bicycle troops would be the new cavalry. No more horses to tend to and manage! But as it turned out, bicycles (and cavalry) proved impractical in static trench warfare.

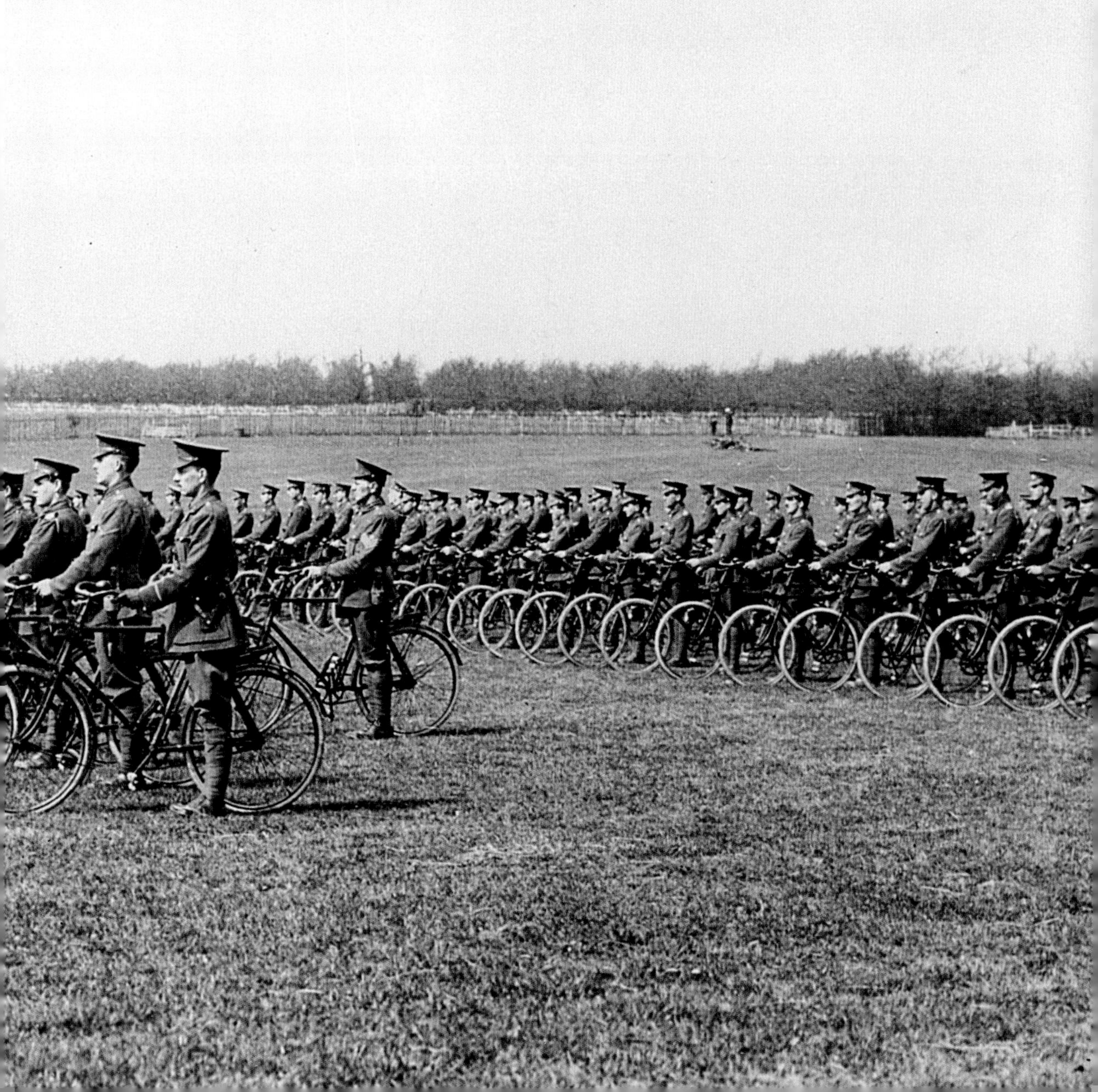

They just don't make adverts like they used to.

This guy is made up to be all alone in a war zone with nothing but his durable Dunlop tyres. Highly useful for self-preservation.

Smoking may eventually kill you, but it may save your life first ... Cigarette cases could act as pocket-sized shields. This **cigarette case** belonged to Rifleman William Stafford Main. He survived the wound inflicted by the shell fragment that pierced the case and, after treatment, returned to active service on the Western Front.

Stories of bibles stopping bullets were quite common in the First World War. This **Bible** saved the life of Gunner John Dickinson, who served in the Royal Horse Artillery. It was in his left breast pocket when he was hit in 1915, and the bullet stopped about a third of the way through the pages.

WEIRD WAR FACT

In the climate of war, superstitions flourished. The diary of Lieutenant F Bass offers some well-founded, if slightly ironic, ones:

- *If the sun rises in the east, it's a sure sign there'll be stew for dinner.*

- *It's considered very unlucky to be killed on a Friday.*

- *Dropping your rifle on the foot of a sergeant major is bad luck.*

- *If you hear a lecture on the glorious history of your regiment, you'll shortly be going over the top.*

Trench signage – not an adornment, but a necessity. The bullet holes in this sign prove its point. But to get close enough to read the warning, presumably you'd have to 'stand about' in the line of fire?

An early health and safety warning, and one it would have been unwise to ignore with German snipers about.

Ah, the clarity of Great British sign makers. All sorts of juvenile jests suggest themselves, but this is in fact a poison gas warning. The wind direction and strength here made it a favourable spot for the enemy to release gas. 'Put on your gas mask' would have been the obvious option.

A place associated with the horrors of trench congestion, or the resting place for large quantities of army-issue Ticklers Plum and Apple Jam?

The trenches were labyrinthine. Troops navigated by way of wooden signs relating to landmarks local to the units that occupied the trenches, or well-known streets and city locations back home. 'Piccadilly Circus' was a popular name for any busy location. This particular sign comes from a defensive trench at Gaza in Palestine — a long way from the pre-war bright lights of the West End.

'Britifying' a bleak setting: conjuring up thoughts of a very far-off home county.

A jolly **Christmas card** from the 4th Division, giving those back home an itchy feel for trench life. Bloodsucking insects were a constant problem. It's estimated that up to 97 per cent of officers and men in the trenches were infested with lice, for example. Men wage war: beasties win, every time.

▼ For many soldiers on active service, personal cleanliness came down to an occasional dip in lukewarm and murky waters in the tub. These were housed in a divisional **bath house**, which was often a requisitioned brewery. No doubt most men would have preferred a tub of beer to wallow in.

A **station for bathing and disinfection** of German troops. The inscription at the door reads: 'Hell where the lice are roasted is heaven for the soldier toasted'.

▼ It may look like an early Casper the Friendly Ghost, but this was a deathly serious bit of headgear. The early British **gas mask**, called the tube or phenate helmet, featured durable glass goggles set on a hood made of multi-layered linen. The helmet was first soaked in sodium phenate, which counteracted the gas, and when worn was tucked securely within the collar of the tunic or greatcoat.

▲ A **leather helmet** with visor and chain mail face mask issued to the first British tank crews in 1916. It was meant to protect the wearer's head from knocks in the constricted interior and his eyes from 'splash', tiny bits of flying metal caused by projectiles hitting the sides of the vehicle. It was later redesigned, partly because it bore an unfortunate resemblance to the German steel helmet — as tank crews forced to abandoned their vehicles sometimes discovered to their cost when they were fired upon by their own side. Can you blame them, with *that* nightmarish vision coming toward them?

▲ The Prussian *Garde du Corps* were the kaiser's personal bodyguards and so of course they needed an impressive **helmet** to make would-be assassins think again. Here it is, topped by a large crowned eagle in silver which was, handily, detachable.

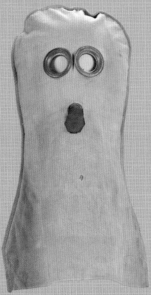

A formal studio **souvenir portrait** from 1914. The gravity of the men in shot suggests they take piloting an imaginary airship very seriously indeed, while the mortified teddy jumps ship.

One of the more unusual souvenirs collected by a solider – a **gargoyle** taken from St Martin's Cathedral in Ypres, Belgium, by Major R J Craig in 1917. Ypres had been shelled to rubble by the Germans, and Winston Churchill urged that it should never be rebuilt to preserve the memory of the war and all the men who had died to protect the town. (He did not, however, urge his troops to slip chunks of stonework in their pockets as mementos.)

A **scrap of wallpaper** from a captured German trench. Fighting a largely defensive war, the Germans could afford to build better trenches with some of the comforts of home, including electric lighting and wallpaper the women back home would have given the thumbs-up.

A Bavarian non-commissioned **officer festooned with flowers.** Bouquets of flowers were handed to departing soldiers by well-wishers. It looks as if this one was at the head of the column, or particularly popular with the ladies.

A popular tradition with German regiments was to take pictures of contrasting soldiers in the regiment and sell them as **souvenir postcards**. Here, Little and Large of the 24th Reserve Division.

Camouflage
and Deception

FROM DAZZLING SHIPS
TO DRAGGED-UP SAILORS

PAGE 38
Hang on, that bush has feet... and a hat! It's a captured **Turkish sniper**, ingeniously screened by a Jack-in-the-Green arrangement of foliage attached to his clothing. Snipers were particularly active in the close-quarter fighting on the peninsula, and the inexperienced troops who landed at Suvla in August 1915 were taken aback by enemy marksmen who fired at them from all angles.

PAGE 39
A Dazzled Merchantman, a 1918 oil painting by Charles Pears of a **dazzle-camouflaged merchant vessel** at sea. Let your eyes drift out of focus a little and the ship merges with the waves it's ploughing through and the backdrop of the leaden sky... Well, at the very least it doesn't look quite as boat-like.

IN THE FIRST WORLD WAR the art of camouflage was still in its infancy. To begin with, many in the military regarded it as cheating to hide soldiers and weapons in the 'game of war'. Trench warfare and aerial reconnaissance soon put paid to that.

In 1914 the German Army went to war in field-grey and the British Expeditionary Force crossed to France in khaki cloth. Unfortunately, France and Belgium missed the memo and strode out in splendidly colourful uniforms, making them easy targets. After many men were indeed shot, the French switched to a muted horizon-blue look and the Belgians went with khaki.

Now camouflage was all the rage. 'Why stop at blending soldiers into the surroundings?' argued a new breed, the *camoufleurs*, who included artists, theatrical scene painters, carpenters and architects. Through nets, screens and paint schemes, they could make a battlefield look deserted, artfully blending machine gun and observation posts and artillery into the landscape.

Concealing the massive machines of war — ships and planes — was trickier. Certainly, throwing a vast camo net over either wasn't going to work. But bamboozling the enemy just might. And so the First World War saw some of the funkiest battleships and planes in history, painted in 'dazzle patterns' that made outline, speed and direction hard to determine.

Bamboozling is an art form to embrace in military warfare. Beyond the camouflage, all sides worked hard to gain the upper hand through the element of surprise. Decoys, dummies and fakes: all designed to distract and confuse the enemy as you delivered the fatal blow... in some cases, wearing a bonnet and dress having posed as a maiden in distress.

A Flower class sloop built in 1917, **HMS *Saxifrage*** was used during 1918 as a Q-ship or anti-sub decoy, and so was painted in dazzle camouflage. She's still afloat today, but bears a different name – as HMS *President* she's prominently and permanently moored on the Thames Embankment in London.

▶ After the war, dazzle pattern became a fashion craze. It even appeared on **swimsuits**, as modelled by this trio on Margate beach in 1920. There was some debate in the newspapers about whether this kind of camouflage swimsuit was more or less revealing than a normal one.

◀ A late-1917 experimental black and white **camouflage outfit** designed to conceal US soldiers while they climbed trees. Unfortunately, he sticks out like a sore thumb in this setting.

▲ A hand-painted **German Storm Troop helmet.** The lozenge pattern breaks up the distinctive profile of the German *stahlhelm*. Helmet painting was a do-it-yourself affair. The soldier/artist here has done a decent job, which may just have saved his life (*may* — there's a pretty big dent in the helmet).

▼ Camo for a pony? Why not. Camouflaged as a zebra, this **pony** could be tethered in the open in German East Africa, where zebra were common. Two white ponies behind anxiously await their makeovers.

British Army **sniper's robe**. Ugly, but effective — in the trenches it was the next best thing to Harry Potter's invisibility cloak.

This is **Mary B Mitchell,** a decoy ship. She carried numerous ingeniously concealed guns that could be fired very quickly – within 11 seconds. Her job was to lure out, and then destroy, the German U-boats that were wreaking havoc among Allied merchant ships. Following an attack by a surfaced enemy sub, a small group called the 'panic party' would theatrically abandon their vessel, leaving the remaining crew to attack the sub when it approached. Sometimes one of the ship's men would wear women's clothing – a dress, a fetching bonnet – in an attempt to draw the Germans closer.

First World War period British **ship model** displaying an
Admiralty 'Type 14G' dazzle-camouflage paint scheme
devised by official War Artist Norman Wilkinson.

Did you ever see such a
funky liner as this model
of **RMS *Mauretania***?
You'd be forgiven for
thinking that the model
maker got carried away,
but in fact this is true
to life: camouflage was
sometimes a surprisingly
colourful business. 'Dazzle'
painting was introduced
as a response to German
U-boat attacks. It relied
on the use of strongly
contrasting blocks of colour
within a special pattern.
The idea was to distort the
outlines of a ship so much that
U-boats would have difficulty
estimating its course and
speed and so were less likely
to aim a torpedo correctly.

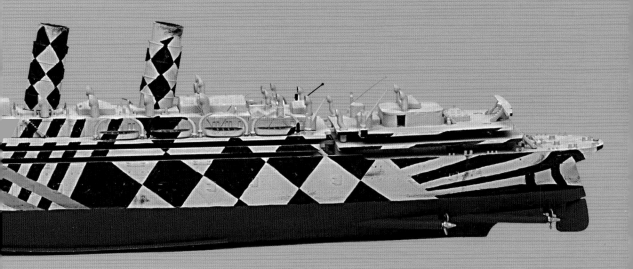

Dazzle camouflage was used on planes too, in this case a British **flying boat** (a Felixstowe F2A) on an anti-submarine patrol. The idea was to aid identification in the air during combat and on the water in the event of being forced down. (Other pilots preferred to take the opposite approach. A German inventor built an 'invisible' fighter with clear cellophane skin. Unfortunately for him, the cellophane reflected sunlight, making it highly visible from a distance.)

Large-scale model of the camouflaged **Gotha G.IV German heavy bomber**. These planes terrorised the citizens of London between May 1917 and May 1918, making 52 raids in which they dropped 105,000 kilograms of high-explosive bombs and 6,500 kilograms of incendiaries.

Rudder from a **German Albatross D3** aircraft. Resembling a piece of modern art, the complex arrangement of lozenge shapes was designed to make outlines and direction of travel more difficult to calculate. But camouflage did not make planes invulnerable. This rudder is likely from an Albatross shot down over the Western Front in November 1917.

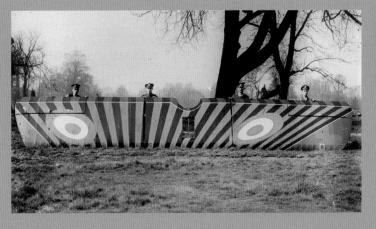

Camouflage on the upper wing of a **Sopwith Camel** fighter. This design creates an optical illusion to deceive enemy airmen as to the centre of the machine, where the pilot sat.

◀ The work of the British Army Camouflage School in Kensington, these **cut-out soldiers** were designed to mislead the enemy during attacks. Could you tell the difference in the heat of the moment and in the murky conditions of the Western Front?

A workshop for assembling **dummy soldiers**. Probably not what the soldiers in shot thought they were signing up for when they joined the Royal Engineers.

▶ Dummy **papier mâché heads**, first made by the French in the winter of 1915, were used to flush out German snipers. For extra realism, in some cases soldiers blew cigarette smoke into a rubber tube leading to the dummy's mouth. In a local attack near Vimy Ridge on the Western Front in November 1917, soldiers went so far as to paint 'the desired effect of heavy enemy fire' on the wooden bodies of their dummies before thrusting them out of the trenches.

▲ The Gallipoli campaign was a disastrous failure, and in December 1915 the Allies wanted out. But they needed a plan to distract the enemy as they withdrew. **Cricket** seemed a most civilised option. So here, Australian troops play a match to distract the (no doubt puzzled) enemy, with Major George Macarthur Onslow of the 7th Light Horse being caught out as shells fly overhead.

Good grief those are strong lads!

No, in fact these Australian Engineers of the 4th Field Company are carrying a **dummy British tank**. Such tanks, made of wood and canvas, were used in an assault on part of the Hindenburg Line in 1918 to confuse the enemy.

▶ A close-up of the back of the same **tree**. As you can see, the chicken wire would hardly have stopped a shell splinter. The soldier within was simultaneously cramped and horribly exposed. All for a good cause, though. Well, so he thought – after the war the verdict was that plenty of the trees were situated where there wasn't much of interest to see.

Spot the real tree...

Here's an 'observation tree' made of canvas and steel, near Souchez, May 1918.

Such trees were used by both the Allies and Germans on the Western Front to conceal observers and snipers. Often, an exact copy of an existing tree (usually dead or shell-damaged) would be made. Under the cover of darkness, the real tree would be removed and carefully replaced with the fake. The hollow within the tree was tight, and tested the nerves of the most enthusiastic and determined of men.

Inventions and Gadgets

FROM WIBBLE-WOBBLES
TO SHIELD SHOVELS

PAGE 54
The solid metal **Brewster Body Shield** was one of the more effective forms of body armour developed in the First World War. The invention could stop machine-gun bullets. Obviously, weight and manoeuvrability were something of an issue...

PAGE 55
Canadian politician Sir Samuel Hughes designed the **MacAdam Shield Shovel**. The idea was to combine a spade with a shield that a soldier could poke his rifle through. Some 20,000 were made before it was discovered that the Shield Shovel wasn't much use as a spade, owing to the large hole in it. Nor was it even slightly bulletproof.

THE FIRST WORLD WAR stimulated vast and unprecedented improvements in existing technologies and the introduction of startling new inventions.

Suddenly, armed forces had at their disposal flame-throwers, machine guns, howitzers and long-range artillery. They could barrel into battle in an armoured tank, attack from on high with all manner of new aircraft, and creep up on battleships and supply vessels in submarines. They could examine decent photographs taken during reconnaissance, and communicate on more reliable telephones.

Behind the lines the supply chain was benefitting from automotive advances and improved railway engines and rolling stock, and pioneering medics were using X-rays, blood transfusions and plastic surgery.

Technology was saving lives — but it was also taking them. The use of the new technologies in firepower, especially the machine gun and quick-firing artillery, helped create a stalemate on the Western Front. The war that many predicted would end by Christmas 1914 took on a life of its own.

Back home, chemists, engineers and specialist scientists were powerhouses of ideas. Some, like the creep tank and the giant periscope, were genius. Others, like the MacAdam Shield Shovel, were total duds. Meanwhile, at the front men improvised their own weapons and gadgets, from jam tin bombs to periscope rifles.

Ultimately, the First World War had become a competition in who had the better technology, as much as who fought the hardest and the cleverest.

The tank was the marvel of the time — alien and futuristic in look. In this **French poster**, the artist portrays the tank, 'the machine to win the war', like an invading Martian from H G Wells' 1897 sci-fi novel *The War of the Worlds*.

THE TANK IS COMING!

HAVE YOUR MONEY ——— READY

SCOTTISH WAR SAVINGS COMMITTEE
90 Princes Street, Edinburgh
(Appointed by H.M. Treasury)

VISIT JULIAN THE TANK

STATIONED AT THE

FOOT OF LEITH WALK

AND BUY

WAR BONDS

£5 to £5000

AND

War Savings Certificates 15/6

Back the tank! The British authorities used the public's fascination with the new wonder weapon as a way of **raising money** for the war. A battered tank named *Egbert* was brought over from France in March 1918 and installed in Trafalgar Square. People bought war bonds and certificates, which were stamped by a young woman who sat inside the tank.

A **home tank (piggy) bank** to incentivise saving for the war effort. 'Where's that blinking kaiser?' wonders this green-glazed ceramic Old Bill.

The **'tank bank'** scheme was so successful that six tanks, including *Julian*, toured the country. Competition between cities to raise the most funds was fierce, and the atmosphere towards the end of each week was likened to that of a cup final.

▶ Meet **Egbert,** the Trafalgar Square tank bank. Poor battle-damaged *Egbert* later featured in an official film, *Tank Trench-Crossing Trials*. He didn't fare well.

WEIRD WAR FACT

The British were the first to use the tank, in 1916. The new weapon was given the codename 'water tank' during development and the name stuck, despite attempts to call them more impressive names such as 'combat cars' and 'assault carriages'. Because the Admiralty's Department of Naval Construction stumped up the money for the initial research and development, tanks were also called 'land ships' and 'land dreadnoughts'.

*First World War slang for the tank included 'boojum', 'land creeper', 'whippet', 'wibble-wobble' and 'Willie'. Many of the crews personalised their machines and gave them names like **Oh I Say!** and **Lusitania.***

▼ In the days before health and safety, an intrepid member of the Imperial War Museum's staff demonstrates a large German **man trap**. These were sometimes used in no man's land.

◀ At the start of the war, the British Army was short of hand grenades. So troops improvised their own. A favourite was the **jam tin bomb** — an old tin filled with nails, metal fragments and explosive. The soldier lit the short fuse with a match and tried to throw it in time before it blew him up. Later, jam tin bombs were commercially manufactured. Pictured here is the No. 8 Mk 1 Jam Tin, made by Roburite & Ammonal Ltd, London, in May 1915.

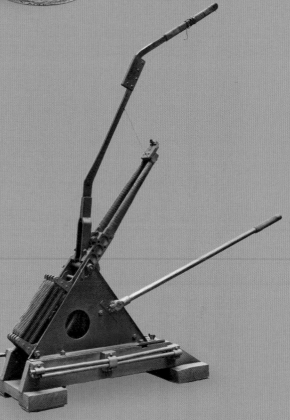

▶ In the early days of trench warfare, specialist weapons like trench mortars were in short supply, and so all armies used new versions of the age-old catapult. This British **West Spring Gun** was designed to hurl fused grenades short distances. But disaster struck if the weapon was wrongly positioned. Then the released grenade would hit the parapet and rebound into the trench — with fatal consequences for both the catapult and its operatives.

A primitive British **periscope rifle mount**, or 'sniperscope', in use on the Western Front in early 1915. The wooden framework allowed the soldier to position the rifle above the trench parapet without the need to expose his head. He used the periscope sight to aim and pulled a string to activate the trigger. Genius – except that the contraption attracted the attention of the enemy and drew fire.

An improvised **spring-loaded gun.** At the end of the war the German High Seas Fleet was interned at Scapa Flow in the Orkney Islands while the Allies decided what to do with it. The sailors had no meat, so they made devices like this to catch supper: sea gulls.

An **ancient invention** pressed into service again. Two semi-circular toothed jaws powered by opposing leaf springs and a chain tether – for all your man-trapping needs.

WEIRD WAR FACT

Exploiting her superb chemical industries, Germany employed poison gas as an alternative to bombardment. It was first used on a mass scale in a major attack at Ypres in April 1915. Allied troops at the mercy of this new weapon improvised crude forms of personal protection, but many succumbed to the chlorine before the German advance was stopped. Subsequently, soldiers were given gas masks, which provided uncomfortable protection (if they could get their masks on fast enough).

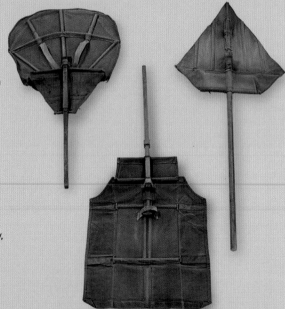

Soon after the first German poison gas attack at Ypres, the British Army called for 'some obstacle which, when oscillated in the air close to our trenches, would set up currents which would, while sending the noxious gases back towards the enemy, at the same time keep our men well supplied with fresh air from behind'. The answer came from Mrs Herta Aryton. It was a **fan on a stick**. Unfortunately, Mrs Aryton's June 1917 'mechanically driven' version was found to be worse than useless in trials.

▶ 'The Blow-bomb for Extinguishing the Fuses of Zeppelin Bombs.' Artist **William Heath Robinson** was legendary for drawing elaborate, absurd inventions. He published two books of these wonder weapons during the conflict, some of them based on suggestions sent in by men in the forces. At one point Heath Robinson even fell foul of the War Office, who thought that one of his pictures showed a genuine military device they were developing. Not the Blow-bomb, clearly.

The Blow-bomb for Extinguishing the Fuses of Zeppelin Bombs

▶ A **giant mobile periscope** being demonstrated at Crystal Palace (the home of the Imperial War Museum between 1920 and 1923) after the war. The Germans used this type of periscope for observing enemy positions and locating targets for the artillery, as well as registering the accuracy of their fire. When fully extended, the periscope could reach up to 25 metres in height, so the user could see over hills and buildings. As long as the wind was light, that is.

▲ Here's a shed that would get a planning officer hot under the collar today: this one was cunningly designed to **conceal a giant periscope**.

◀ A daring way to gather information intel: a Royal Field Artillery spotter in Mesopotamia balances precariously atop a **'limber pole ladder'**. At least he has the protection of a thin metal shield; more than the range-finder immediately below him. The flat desert terrain of parts of Mesopotamia meant that even a modest boost in height could really help with reconnaissance.

▲ An inspiration for Mickey Mouse? The most likely explanation for this strange **headgear**, worn by two members of the Imperial German Army, is that it helped the wearer pinpoint the position of enemy guns, possibly by enhancing the booms and flashes.

▲ A **British Mark 1 Sound Locator**. Before the invention of radar, those on the lookout for Zeppelins or bombers would use these giant ear trumpets to listen for approaching aircraft.

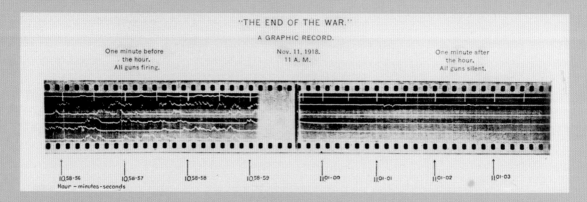

"THE END OF THE WAR."

A GRAPHIC RECORD.

One minute before
the hour.
All guns firing.

Nov. 11, 1918.
11 A.M.

One minute after
the hour.
All guns silent.

10.58-56 10.58-57 10.58-58 10.58-59 11.01-00 11.01-01 11.01-02 11.01-03

Hour – minutes–seconds

▶ Ciphers — a means of encoding by substituting letters according to a key — have been around a long time. Julius Caesar sent secret messages to his armed forces this way. Over time ciphers got more sophisticated and more difficult to decode. The **Pletts enciphering machine** was very cunning and its inventor, a radio engineer, was sure the code created was pretty unbreakable. However, the device unfortunately failed its trials and was never adopted by the British Army.

▲ The French developed a way of recording **sound signals** onto film, which helped them to plot accurately the position of enemy guns by calculating the time between the noise of a shell firing and its explosion. This piece of film records one minute before and one minute after the end of the war. You can see the trace go flat as the guns fall silent at 11am on 11 November 1918.

▶ An Austrian gadget for working out the correct **rate of march**. You placed the two pointers on a map and the overlapping leaves gave an indication of how long it would take troops to cover that distance at their standard rate of march. This clever contraption also gave details of the length of column they would form. All that from some pointy metal!

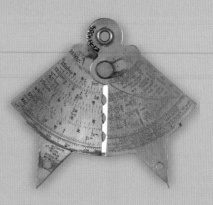

American sailors wearing mattresses

designed to double as lifejackets in case they had to abandon ship. A buoyant mattress – the precursor of the lilo?

Flight

FROM PARASITE PLANES TO
RANDY RICHARDS

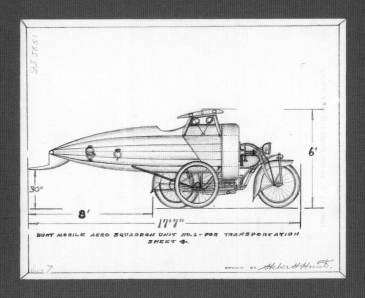

HUNT MOBILE AERO SQUADRON UNIT NO.1 - FOR TRANSPORTATION
SHEET 4.

DRAWN BY Hubert H. Hunt

PAGE 68
An eight-foot-high **landing wheel** from Germany's Poll Giant Triplane, an unfinished aircraft discovered in a hangar after the war. This ten-engined monster was originally thought to have been a bomber, designed to cross the ocean and attack New York. More recent research suggests that the Poll Giant was intended as a long-range transport aircraft. The aircraft was so huge — the span of the centre wing was 50.3 metres — that it probably wouldn't have got airborne, and some people reckon its construction was for a propaganda stunt.

THE FIRST WORLD WAR transformed aviation. At the outset of war, 'air power' was represented by observation balloons and flimsy, slow, unreliable aeroplanes employed for reconnaissance. By the war's end, heavily armed fast-flying fighters ruled the skies and gigantic long-range bombers delivered payloads of a previously unimaginable scale. For the first time in history, the sky itself became a battlefield.

It was developments in aerial photography and air-to-ground communications that changed the game. Now pilots could pass accurate information on the enemy to artillery and infantry units on the ground. Gone was the friendly waving between opposing air crews. Instead, they sought to take down the enemy — at first with shotgun and pistol, and later with machine guns fitted to the aircraft. Air fighting tactics evolved, and expert pilots — 'aces' — became renowned for their skill and audacity. .

Meanwhile, designers and engineers were locked up in workshops developing The Next Big Thing in aeronautics. Some inventions were brilliant — and deadly — like the German Zeppelin that terrorised cities in Belgium, France and England, and the huge fixed-wing bomber aircraft created to retaliate. Others were incredibly innovative, such as radio-controlled drones, rocket armaments and parasite planes. Still others, like the Man-Carrying Kite and the Poll Giant Triplane, were firmly in the wacky camp.

By the end of the war, sophisticated flying machines existed in their thousands, and many more were in development. Leaders had acknowledged that control of the air was essential for successful military operations, and a terrible precedent had been set for all ensuing major conflicts.

PAGE 69

Just after the First World War, Herber H Hunt submitted these **plans** to the US Army. They showed how you could split 13 aeroplanes up into sections and attach them to motorbikes to create a 'Mobile Aero Squadron'. Herber was serving a five-year sentence in military prison for unauthorised use of federal property at the time, and he hoped this was his get-out-of-jail-free card. Apparently the US Army was interested, but there's no record of whether the squadron were developed — or, indeed, of whether Herber had engineered his freedom.

▶ Pilot **Manfred von Richtofen's room** decorated with trophies of his victories, including serial numbers cut from British planes and a captured British engine turned into a chandelier. The Red Baron, as he was named after his trademark red triplane, was the most famous and successful fighter 'ace' of the war, shooting down 80 planes. The unit he led — the *Richthofen Jagdgeshwader* (or Fighter Wing) — was nicknamed the Flying Circus because of its colourful planes and all the men and lorries required to move the unit to different sectors of the front.

Plane spotter heaven: here's a public warning **poster** from 1915 helping British civilians to spot the difference between British and German aircraft. So they knew whether to wave or run.

Despite their logic and technical skills, pilots could be very superstitious and would often wear or carry **lucky charms**. Here's a metal charm of an aeroplane.

Another **charm** (jewellery makers clearly saw the potential). These are so tiny – drop one in the cockpit and you'd have no luck finding your lucky charm.

WEIRD WAR FACT

US pilot Howard Clayton Knotts shot down six German planes in a month in 1918. That was remarkable, but his real claim to fame is the number of planes he destroyed once he got shot down himself. After being hit, he landed behind German lines and was transferred to a POW camp by train. While on the train he discovered that seven Fokker aircraft were in a freight car on their way to an aerodrome. When the train stopped, Knotts managed to set fire to the carriage the planes were in, destroying the lot.

WEIRD WAR FACT

*The rotary engines that powered Allied First World War
fighters used pharmaceutical-quality castor oil for lubrication.
Unfortunately, the pilots 'benefited' from this remedy when they
swallowed oil that continually leaked out of the engines.
The result: persistent diarrhoea.*

Behold the **parasite plane**, devised by the British in their fight against the Zeppelins. The hope was that a fighter could hitch a ride on another plane and reach a speed and altitude where it could intercept high-flying Zepps. In May 1916 an experiment saw a Bristol Scout fighter attach to a Porte Baby flying boat. Someone had forgotten to factor in weight, though: the added 'parasite' made the flying boat burn through fuel, so it couldn't make it as far as Zepp flight paths.

Sopwith Triplane single-seat fighting scout. This fighter performed exceptionally well, holding its own against German fighters in early 1917. It was affectionately known as the Tripehound and was much used by Royal Naval Air Service squadrons. Its success inspired the Germans to introduce triplane fighters later that year.

Most First World War planes had two sets of wings rather than the single set we're used to today. Doubling the number of wings meant more lift and manoeuvrability – crucial in dogfights. The downside was lack of speed. That didn't stop the manufacturer creating triplanes and then quadruplanes. Pictured here is the **Pemberton Billing Supermarine Night Hawk**. Sounds brilliantly powerful and speedy, doesn't it? Actually, the plane was more duck than hawk. It struggled to reach 60 miles per hour and took an hour to reach 10,000 feet – not ideal for a plane designed to fight high-flying Zeppelins.

In the last month of the war, the British had another stab at the parasite plane, and successfully released a **Sopwith Camel** fighter from an airship. But this time someone had forgotten the aim of the exercise: to convey a fighter to a location and altitude at which the pilot could launch an attack on enemy airships. The released parasite Sopwith Camel was pilotless. Strike two, and you're out.

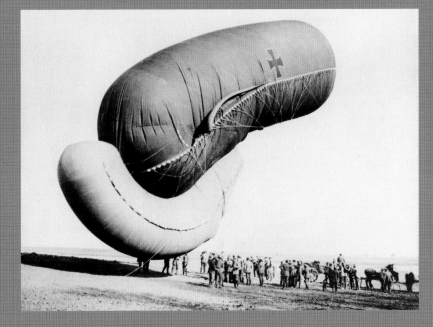

Introducing the *Drachen* (Dragon). No explanations required for why this early German **observation balloon** was nicknamed the Sausage. The oddly shaped appendage at rear-underside of the craft was an air rudder, designed to improve the stability of the balloon in strong winds. The bun, if you like, to the hotdog.

Did you know that unmanned drones were first pioneered in the First World War?

They were — just not very successfully. The **Sopwith Aerial Target** of 1917 was a miniature radio-controlled plane packed with explosives that was designed to be steered into Zeppelins. Its inventor, the self-styled 'Professor' Archibald Low, was a pioneer in radio guidance systems, but unfortunately he knew less about building aircraft. When the drone was demonstrated to a group of generals it failed to take off and instead veered and barrelled along the ground towards them, nearly wiping them out.

In a **later test** the Sopwith Aerial Target did at least take off, but only to loop the loop and hit the ground.

Designed to enable the 'pilot' to survey the battlefield and signal enemy positions, the Perkins Man-Carrying Kite of 1915.

It was named in the spirit of 'does what it says on the tin', but failed to deliver on the 'kite' aspect: it stalled at the testing stage. A case of 'Let's *Not* Go Fly a Kite.'

WEIRD WAR FACT

Weather permitting, large observation balloons were tethered to the ground at intervals of a mile or so close behind the lines. Beneath each balloon, which resembled a giant floating marrow, a 'balloonatic' sat in a basket, keeping a lookout. The British called these balloons Randy Richards.

Two soldiers of the Hampshire Regiment releasing **balloons** to which they've attached bundles of propaganda leaflets (near Bethune, September 1918). All sides used balloons to spread propaganda leaflets. All sides did not, however, sport such high-waisted shorts held up with braces.

A *spähkorb* or **spy basket** (also called a cloud car) from a Zeppelin. Zeppelins could fly well above the clouds, and when they did so, in order to navigate and direct bombs, the crew lowered this device on a cable. An intrepid crew member dangled anything up to half a mile below the airship in the *spähkorb*, giving instructions over a telephone. To reduce the discomfort, some spy baskets were equipped with a wicker chair, table and lamp (and lightning conductor). Crew members would volunteer because it was the only place they could 'safely' smoke.

Communication

FROM TEACH-YOURSELF SEMAPHORE
TO MULTIPLE-CHOICE POSTCARDS

PAGE 82
A cheery **artilleryman** with the post for his battery, near Aveluy on the Somme, September 1916. The British Army Postal Service, operated by the Royal Engineers, was highly efficient (more so than today's post): on average it took two days for a letter posted in Britain to reach its destination on the Western Front. The parcels this postie is balancing most likely contained food – not a single morsel would be wasted by men living on army rations.

PAGE 83
Why train troops in semaphore signalling when they can teach themselves? According to these British Army **instructional cards**, a dedicated student would master the skill in a matter of hours. Not the sort of cards you would expect to be popular with soldiers.

GOOD COMMUNICATIONS are vital for success in warfare. In the First World War, advances in telegraph and telephone communications were novel and promising – but shellfire easily decimated the wires. Flags, signal lamps and heliographs (wireless solar telegraph) were well-established – but useless in smoke and rain. So armed forces frequently had to fall back on age-old communication methods like signal rockets, runners, carrier pigeons and messenger dogs.

This new 'fog of war' stimulated rapid technological developments in the field of wireless technology. Imagine how game-changing it was in 1915 when pilots could actually radio artillery on the ground, rather than dropping a scribbled note from on high!

But communication wasn't all about military operations – it was about boosting morale by helping servicemen to keep in touch with loved ones back home. The postal service was surprisingly efficient and operated at a speed we might envy today.

The extraordinary amounts of correspondence proved a test for the intelligence agencies, and censors had their work cut out checking that men weren't accidentally letting slip sensitive information to Aunt Ethel back home. 'How's the weather?' was just about the only safe topic of conversation. The answer, invariably, for the men in the trenches: 'Dismal'.

Still, there was fun to be had with the game of the times, 'Beat the Censor'. Both servicemen and civilians found ways around the rules, writing in code and hiding messages in commonplace objects. Biscuit love letter, anyone?

A Great Eastern Railway Company driver on a battery-powered **Railodok parcel truck** (1917). Given the teetering load and her precarious position on the driver's perch, an emergency stop must have proved painful.

A dance class?
No, flag
**semaphore
signalling**
instruction at
Fort Blockhouse,
Portsmouth
Harbour.
Prior to radio
communication,
signalling flags
and lamps were
the means
for inter-ship
communication.

September 1916, and a rare dry day on the Western Front. A **heliograph signal station** has been set up on King George's Hill, near Fricourt on the Somme. The hill was named after King George V's visit to Fricourt (when he was filmed by the official cinematographer) and the emblem on the board is the red rose of the 55th (West Lancashire) Division.

KING GEORGES HILL.

Sitting in a field, pedalling and going... nowhere. The Germans sometimes used **pedal power** to generate electricity for communications and lights during the First World War.

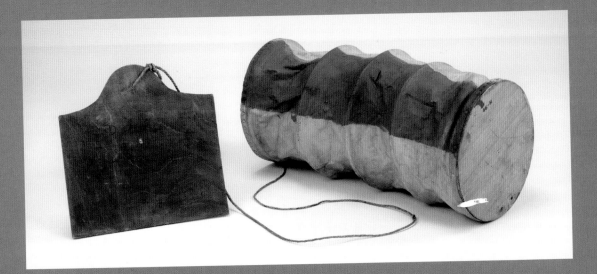

Message drogue (small parachute) with message board. The pilot of a French seaplane dropped this message alongside HMS *Marksman* on 21 June 1918: 'Attacked enemy submarine at 11.20am, 18 miles N25W from Dunkirk, proceeding to the west.' Prior to the radio, message dropping was the only way a pilot could communicate with the ground.

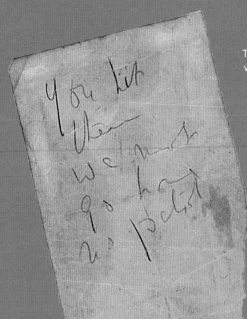

This hastily scribbled **message** was thrown from a British aircraft onto an artillery battery on the Western Front in October 1914. It reads succinctly: 'You hit them. We must go home. No petrol.'

The unpalatable hardness of the standard-issue **army ration biscuit** encouraged all sorts of creativity in the field kitchen. Here, it serves as a Christmas card.

A French **slang phrasebook** for British troops, handy when dealing with Allied troops and local civilians. Includes translations for all the essential vocabulary a serviceman could need, from the verbs to swank (*faire de l'éparte*), to dodge the column (*se trotter*), to scrounge (*chiper*), to lark about (*rigoler*) and to save one's bacon (*sauver sa pean*), to the declaration 'I am fed up' (*J'en ai soupé*).

A **letter hidden inside a walnut shell** baked into a loaf of bread. It was sent to a German prisoner of war in France by his brother. Given the food shortages in Germany (a consequence of the Allied blockade), this was generous as well as inventive.

NOTHING is to be written on this side except the date and signature of the sender. Sentences not required may be erased. If anything else is added the post card will be destroyed.

[Postage must be prepaid on any letter or post card addressed to the sender of this card]

I am quite well.

I have been admitted into hospital

{ sick } and am going on well.

{ wounded } and hope to be discharged soon.

I am being sent down to the base.

I have received your { letter dated _____
{ telegram „ _____
{ parcel „ _____

Letter follows at first opportunity.

I have received no letter from you

{ lately
{ for a long time.

Signature only }

Date_____

Wt.W65—P.P.948. 8000m. 5-18. C. & Co., Grange Mills, S.W.

Document.582/A

Soldiers were allowed to send two letters home per week free of charge. But writing a letter that made sense after your officer censored it was tricky. The officers, meanwhile, didn't much enjoy spending hours checking for accidentally leaked military secrets amid personal chitchat. The solution: **Field Service postcards**. With a simple tick, you could complete a pre-censored postcard to convey essential information. Such a delicate way to tell your girl back home that you're wounded and in hospital.

XMAS, 1916. THE DUMP.

A LONG-FELT WANT.

We have often felt that the Field Service Post Card, excellent though it be, does not offer sufficient scope for the expression of the different circumstances in which the British Soldier may find himself. We therefore beg to offer the following suggestions to those whose business it is :—

I am in
- the trenches.
- the pink.
- hospital.
- the soup.
- the guard room.

We have not been paid for
- a week.
- a fortnight.
- a month.

I hope to get leave
- this year.
- next year.
- sometime.
- never.

We are living on
- bully and biscuits.
- biscuits and bully.
- bully.
- biscuits.

Gott strafe the War.

From your loving
- son.
- husband.
- sweetheart.
- brother.
- father.
- grandfather.
- great-grandfather.

Signature only

The **Field Service Postcard** was begging to be **parodied**. Here's one response from the trench journal *The Dump* in Christmas 1916.

An alternative to the Field Service Postcard was the **Green Honour Envelope**, on which the writer signed a declaration that the letter within didn't give away military secrets. Perfect for love letters. Your letter may be opened at the army base, but not with the battalion, so at least you could look your officer in the eye.

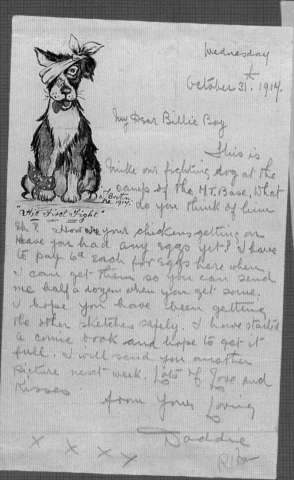

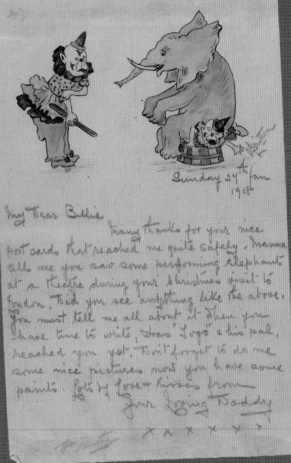

These **illustrated letters** were created by W L Britton while he was on active service in Salonika (northern Greece) between 1917 and early 1919. A former regular soldier, Britton re-enlisted in 1914 as a private in the Army Service Corps.

He left behind a wife and young son but was determined to keep in touch. The letters to his son Billy are funny, bright and optimistic, and they bring to life a too-often forgotten front at Salonika, described as the place where the ultimate collapse of the Central Empires began.

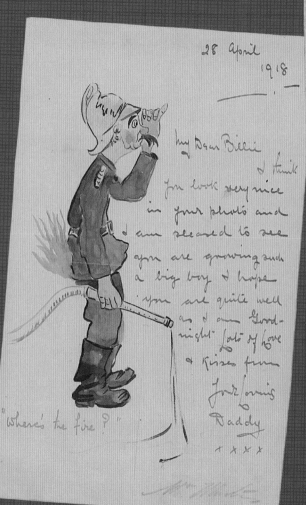

28 April
1918

My Dear Billie
          I think
you look very nice
in your photo and
I am pleased to see
you are growing such
a big boy & hope
you are quite well
as I am. Good-
night. Lots of Love
& Kisses from
Your loving
Daddy
xxxx

"Where's the fire?"

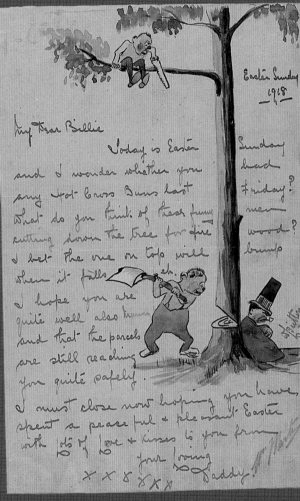

Easter Sunday
1918

My Dear Billie
          Today is Easter
and I wonder whether you
any Hot Cross Buns last
what do you think of these funny
cutting down the tree for fire
I bet the one on top will
when it falls ...eh.
I hope you are
quite well also Mamma
and that the parcels
are still reaching
you quite safely.
I must close now hoping you have
spent a peaceful & pleasant Easter
with lots of Love & Kisses to you from
your loving
x x x x x x   Daddy!

Sunday
had
Friday?
mean
wood?
bump

Spies and
Secret Messages

FROM BIRD-DROPPING INVISIBLE
INK TO TOENAIL ENGRAVINGS

PAGE 96
Towards the end of the war, the Americans began to use members of the **Choctaw Indian tribe** to befuddle Germans eavesdropping on their communications. Because most Native American languages had never been written down, the Germans couldn't understand what Choctaws were saying to each other. The Choctaw language didn't have words for modern weapons, so they improvised, using 'big gun' to describe 'artillery' and 'little gun shoot fast' for 'machine gun'.

PAGE 97
A box of **cigars** sent to Willem Roos and Haicke Janssen, intercepted by MI5 and examined for secret messages. In 1915 the two Dutchmen were posing as cigar salesmen and sending naval intelligence to their German controllers using a code based on cigar orders. Lots of orders. But few sailors smoked cigars; they generally smoked cigarettes or pipes. Busted.

THROUGHOUT THE HISTORY of warfare accurate knowledge of the enemy has proved vital. Reconnaissance patrols gather the most obvious information, but what about delving deeper? Enter the spy: a non-military agent adept at quietly blending into a location, looking, listening, and reporting back covertly.

Spies operated undercover, but their work was infamous. People believed an extensive network of covert 'observers' existed across Europe. In fact, there weren't all that many – and of those operating, few were engaged in exciting, glamorous work.

In the days before hard core spy training, plenty of spies were more inept Johnny English than expert James Bond. For example, German attempts to spy in Britain weren't that successful. At the outbreak of war, the British Secret Service Bureau arrested 21 German agents it had been tracking. To fill the gaps, the Germans sent replacements, but they were undertrained and prone to bumbling.

The authorities used various means to hunt for spies. In Britain, the Postal Censorship Department (MI9) was established, and its painstaking scrutiny of communications led to the downfall of many enemy agents. Meanwhile, clever clogs broke secret codes and technicians in chemical laboratories exposed messages written in invisible ink.

But when it came to spy spotting, Joe Public had the biggest role to play. And they took to it with gusto. Check out the lights in that barn; off, on – surely a secret code! That chap has a camera, and he's asking questions – I spy a spy! Sometimes, the hunch was proved right. But frequently enthusiastic citizens' arrests were to the distress of blameless civilians and genuine journalists. Still, better to be safe than sorry.

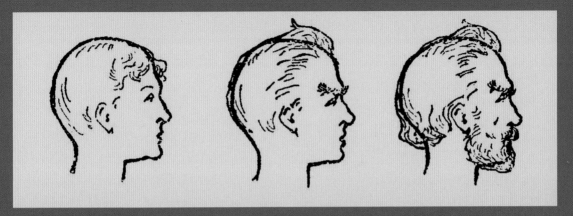

In 1915 the military hero and founder of the Scout movement, **Robert Baden-Powell**, published *My Adventures as a Spy*. The book is a memoir of his espionage activities in the late nineteenth century, when he went on spying missions disguised as a butterfly hunter, an artist and a plumber. Here, Baden-Powell gives a lesson on hairstyling for the would-be spy.

Change gait, change character, claimed Baden-Powell. Gait, he believed, said a lot about a person. In his **1933 autobiography** he claimed that 'about forty-six per cent of women [are] very adventurous with one leg and hesitant on the other, i.e. liable to act on impulse'. How this many women managed to walk without lolloping is a mystery.

BEWARE

—OF—

FEMALE SPIES

Women are being employed by the enemy to secure information from Navy men, on the theory that they are less liable to be suspected than male spies. Beware of inquisitive women as well as prying men.

SEE EVERYTHING
HEAR EVERYTHING
SAY NOTHING
Concerning any matter bearing upon the work of the Navy

SILENCE IS SAFETY

Introducing **Mata Hari**, notorious First World War spy. After a failed marriage, she launched a career as an exotic dancer in Paris, and her sensuous dancing and revealing costumes attracted numerous lovers, including aristocrats and military officers. With her pick of companions, she gave up dancing in favour of a life as a free-spirited courtesan. Seeing that she was ideally placed to gather information, the French employed her as an agent. But the Germans had the same idea. She was arrested by the French, found guilty of being a double-agent and executed by firing squad in October 1917.

The drama surrounding the trial and execution of Mata Hari fuelled the fears of female traitors and spies. This US **poster** warns American men to beware inquisitive women.

Britain's overseas spies were managed by **Captain Mansfield Smith-Cumming**, an eccentric whose trademarks included wearing a gold-rimmed monocle and zooming down corridors with his wooden leg resting on a child's scooter. He would plunge a penknife into his wooden leg as a way of testing potential recruits, telling anyone who flinched, 'Well, you won't do'. Smith-Cumming's office was equally dramatic. To gain entry, his secretary pressed a button to ring a secret bell and Smith-Cumming operated a series of levers and pedals to reveal the entrance.

WEIRD WAR FACT

The British Secret Service Bureau was formed in 1909 (the year that saw the worldwide publication of over 20 spy or invasion scare literary works). The Bureau initially comprised two sections – Home and Foreign, which would subsequently become MI5 and MI6. In 1914 its employees numbered just 19: nine army officers, three civilians, four women clerks and three police detectives.

Inside the Lines very successfully exploited the spy mania of the early years of the war. Set in August 1914, the action centred on Gibraltar – one of the fortress ports of the British Mediterranean Fleet – and the dangers posed by an enemy intent on getting 'inside the lines' of the Rock's formidable defences. Sounds pretty gloomy, but it was marketed as a comedy with mystery and thrill. It was written by Earl Derr Biggers, creator of the Chinese Private Detective Charlie Chan.

This **camera** (a Nettel Argus Monocular of 1911) cunningly takes snaps at right-angles to where the camera is pointing. Such cameras were believed to be popular with German spies in Britain.

A **selection of items** (including a sponge, a bar of soap and a sock) tested by MI5 for invisible ink. They belonged to the German spy Georg Breeckow, who operated in Britain under the alias Reginald Rowland.

WEIRD WAR FACT

In the first year of the war, spy-mania reached fever pitch. Among the many strange ideas that took hold at this time was one that German agents had built specially strengthened tennis courts across London that could be converted to gun emplacements for the invading troops. Equally, spies were rumoured to be leaving instructions on the back of enamelled metal advertisements for Maggi Soup, inspiring groups of patriotically minded citizens to go around unscrewing them to check for foul play.

WEIRD WAR FACT

Paranoia about spies led to a bizarre episode where a lady's maid was strip-searched on leaving the country and found to have 'secret writing' on her bottom. She was arrested and photographs of the writing were sent to German military intelligence for analysis. It turned out that the maid had used the toilet on the train on the way to the border and, worried that the seat might be dirty, had covered it with a newspaper before sitting down. The 'secret writing' was an imprint of the **Frankfurter Zeitung**. *A case of headline news going bottom-up?*

Pills concealed in American magazine *The World's Work Advertiser* taken from a captured German spy. Are they suicide pills? Unlikely given the number (just one does the job). Most likely these are the base for invisible ink.

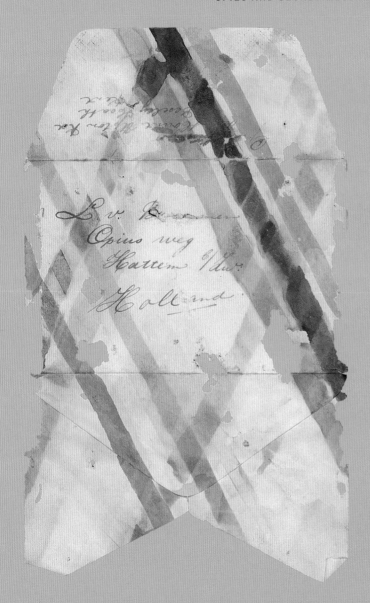

Tin of **talcum powder** found in the possession of the spy Georg Breeckow at the time of his arrest. Innocent enough, you may think, but as the label fixed to the tin states, he used the powder to make invisible ink.

An **envelope** found in possession of a German spy and tested for invisible ink. The envelope is stained with ink or reagent, a substance used in a chemical reaction to detect hidden messages.

A **sheet of music** covered with secret writing, intercepted by British postal censors in July 1915. It was one of four sheets posted to Norway by 'Cecil', real name Courtenay de Rysbach. The hidden text gave detailed information about the British war effort, including possible military targets for German aircraft. On this particular page 'Cecil' asks for more money so that he can pay his brother for information about British naval movements. In October 1915, de Rysbach was sentenced to life imprisonment.

CONFIDENTIAL

REGRADED ~~SECRET~~
Authority: NNØ 750065
By CB/9I NARS, Date MARCH 15,
1976

EXEMPT from automatic declassification
per. E.O. 11552, Sec. 5(E)(2)

Turner	CIA	28 JAN 1978
Name	Agency	Date
A	/	2020
Reason		Review on:
C 78-4 pgt.		

SECRET WRITING

For Secret Writing can be used :

First :   A solution of nitrate of seda and starch in water x
/may be carried for example in handkerchiefs or starched
collars, starched shirts or anything else starched. These
things being laid in this solution and then ironed. The
article thus treated is later on again put in water and
a solution obtained which can be used for invisible
writing. /   The best means for devloping are iodite of
potassium.

Second: Sulphate of iron, developed preferably with ferro
cyanite of potassium.

Third: Nitrate of silver developed preferably with 2,
or 4.

Fourth: Rice starch, developed with ink mixed with water.

Fifth: Lemon juice, developed with Ferro cyanite of potas.

x   A tumbler of water is boiled together with a table spoon
of starch, allow to cool, and add ten gramms of nitrite
of soda.

        For developing secret writing is used:

1.   Iodite of Potassium, /5 grams with 100 grams of water, 2 g
of tartaric acid added/

2.   Sulpharated soda.

3.   Ferro cyanite of potassium.

4.   Ink, mixed with water / laid on with a brush/

APPROVED FOR RELEASE DATE: 31-Mar-2011

A **document** from 1918 listing some of the chemicals and techniques used to create secret writing. It's one of several papers about invisible ink that the CIA finally declassified in 2011. Another is a memorandum from Theodore Kytka, a San Francisco handwriting expert, describing a way of painting invisible messages on the human body. He also warns of other methods that spies may use, including 'placing writings under postage stamps, wrapping messages in medicine capsules and engraving messages... on toenails'.

Animals

FROM PARACHUTING PIGEONS TO
LUMINOUS SEA LIONS

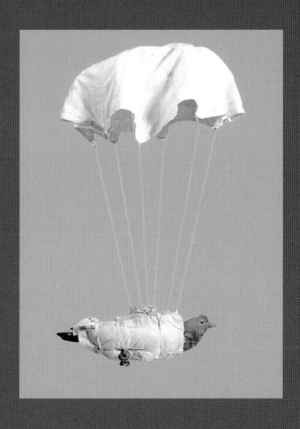

WHILE SERVING WITH the 22nd Royal Fusiliers, the famous animal lover and short-story writer H H Munro (better known as Saki) whimsically identified the badger and the bison as the two animals most perfectly suited to the mud and squalor of the Western Front. Sadly, the contributions of both creatures to victory remain unrecorded. But we do know plenty about the 16 million other animals employed in and behind the battle zones, on all fronts, that lent their (considerable!) weight to the military effort.

Since ancient times, animals — elephants, horses, mules, camels and dogs — have stood shoulder to shoulder (or knee) with men in war. During the First World War horses, mules and camels were key to strategic and logistical goals, transporting vital resources right up to the front line. And on the subject of vital resources, Allied ships groaned under the weight of the fodder and water required for these animals.

Meanwhile, pigeons zipped back and forth overhead, carrying essential messages (and, in some cases, cameras), and in the ocean glowing sea lions hunted U-boats. On land, animals were used to relay information, medicine and ammunition, to stand guard and to locate missing soldiers. Ever-loyal dogs, mostly, but also... a baboon?

Above all, animals were a source of much-needed friendship for troops as pets and mascots. A serviceman may kill an enemy soldier on sight, yet in a heartbeat he'd rescue and care for a creature caught up in the violence of war, be it a dog, a cat, a hedgehog, a pig... or a crocodile!

ON FRIENDLY TERMS WITH ITS COMMANDING OFFICER :
A SEA-LION ON BOARD A SUBMARINE.

A **sea lion** undergoing training to locate submarines off the south coast of Britain. As the war continued German submarines (U-boats) were sinking more and more British supply ships, threatening to starve the nation into surrender. Suggestions for defence measures included stopping subs with giant magnets and training seagulls to defecate on their periscopes. So, the idea of using sea lions seemed relatively sensible. The idea was to train the famously greedy animals to associate submarines with being fed (the Pavlov's seal effect?). Unfortunately, keeping track of the sea lions in the water proved impossible, especially at night, despite the idea of covering them with luminous paint. The plan was scrapped after less than a year in favour of the hydrophone, an underwater microphone. Effective, but much less fun.

Captain Joseph Woodward had achieved fame before the war for teaching sea lions to play the banjo and ride a motorbike in a stage act. But he remained most proud of his role in helping the Admiralty train sea lions to help the war effort, featuring it on his headed notepaper and even his gravestone.

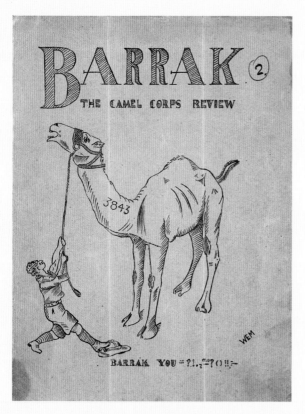

The front cover of the **magazine** *Barrak: The Camel Corps Review* for September 1917, printed in Cairo as the 'official organ' of the Imperial Camel Corps. The camel was an indispensable working animal, but could prove fractious and obstinate. So much so that the word 'camel', said with feeling, became a curse. 'Camel Corps' also doubled as army slang for the infantry, reflecting the heavy loads foot soldiers were required to carry (no doubt while cursing 'camel' under their breath).

Colonel T E Lawrence's camel Ghazala and calf, possibly at Akaba. Colonel Lawrence's Arab forces fully exploited the camel, the grumpy beast of burden perfectly designed to cope with desert conditions. Lawrence himself (like Peter O'Toole, the actor who was later to depict him in the epic 1962 film *Lawrence of Arabia*) did not find learning to ride a camel easy, but eventually he became an accomplished rider.

A hint of the complications wrought by chemical warfare: a Royal Engineer carefully attaches a message to a carrier pigeon safely enclosed in its **gas-proof box**, which looks as straightforward as juggling frogs.

▼ Ferocious German **carrier pigeons**, carefully guarded by their jubilant captors, are displayed in a patriotic parade in the USA.

Tanks were the 'modern wonder weapons' of the First World War, yet their communications systems were anything but wondrous. So troops often relied on **pigeons** to communicate with base. Unfortunately the toxic engine fumes sometimes stupefied the birds (hopefully the bird in this picture flew rather than plummeted). Ships and aeroplanes also routinely carried pigeons to report their locations in case of attack.

▶ Need a bird's eye view? Use a bird... That was the logic of the German military forces who, early in the war, trialled using **pigeons for aerial reconnaissance**. Each bird wore an aluminium breast harness on which a lightweight time-delayed miniature camera was attached. Did these feathered 'eyes in the sky' inspire the future use of robotic flying drones?

WEIRD WAR FACT

In Paris, parrots were positioned in the Eiffel Tower in the hope that, with their superior sense of hearing, they would give a 20-minute warning of the enemy approaching ('Squawk, Polly spies a plane...'). The scheme was dropped after it emerged the parrots could not tell the difference between Allied and German engines!

Miniature dugouts for the French 6th Army's dogs at Gournay, September 1915. Each canine soldier had a small splinter-proof dugout with sandbag protections at the entrance.

By 1917 Britain and France had nearly 20,000 dogs serving, while Germany had nearly 30,000. Any of these wartime dogs would have impressed the judges of *Britain's Got Talent:* they carried messages, stood as sentries and guards, and helped to lay communication cables.

▶ Here's a furry tea trolley: a **dog** fitted with a special harness **delivering dinner** to German troops in an advanced position on the Western Front. The German Army also used dogs to carry ammunition and grenades — not an animal you'd want to pet. Meanwhile the American troops quite happily received small dogs bearing free cigarettes courtesy of the YMCA.

WEIRD WAR FACT

The man in charge of the British War Dog School,
Major Edwin Richardson, felt that almost any
dog was suitable for service as long it had didn't
have 'a gaily carried tail'. This showed 'a certain
levity of character, quite at variance with
the serious duties required'.

When not keeping skulls intact, a **shrapnel helmet** served an excellent secondary use: handy carrier for a soldier's best friend (December 1917).

The Marine Corps claim that their nickname *Teufel Hunden* (Devil Dogs) was applied in grudging admiration by their German opponents following the Marines' furious fighting on the Western Front at Belleau Wood in June 1918. The name and vivid animal symbolism – the German sausage dog pursued by the American Pit Bull Terrier – were vigorously employed by **US poster** artists for recruitment and propaganda purposes.

An inspiration for Hugh Lofting's 1920 book *The Story of Doctor Dolittle*? This **British officer of the Army Veterinary Corps** in Salonika counted among his pets two jackdaws, a wild goose, a wolf cub and an Alsatian dog.

Albert Marr and Jackie the Baboon, starring in the Lord Major's Show in London, 1918. When Private Albert Marr joined the 3rd South African Infantry in 1915, he brought Jackie along with him. It soon became clear Jackie was not aping about; he behaved like one of the team, even saluting officers. So the baboon was made an official member of the regiment. While serving in Egypt, Jackie's sharp senses helped to warn of enemy attack and he nursed an injured Albert back to health. But during fighting in France in 1918 Jackie was wounded in the leg, and he and Albert were released from military duty. They returned to England, where they fund-raised for sick and wounded soldiers. A year later, Jackie was officially discharged, his uniform bearing one gold wound stripe and three blue service chevrons, indicating three years of front line service. He received the usual discharge papers as well as a military pension.

'We saw something making a lot of fuss in the water. It turned out to be a pig from the *Dresden* which had managed to keep afloat. A couple of men dived in and brought it on board... It is bathed every day, and on Sundays wears an iron cross round its neck.' So begins the story of **Tirpitz the pig**, rescued by the sailors of HMS *Glasgow* from the German cruiser *Dresden* that was sunk in March 1915 off the coast of Chile. She became surely the most expensive pig in Britain when the Duke of Portland auctioned and then re-purchased her three times over, raising a total of £68,000 for British war charities.

A sailor relaxes with Tirpitz, so-named after the head of the German Navy, Admiral Alfred von Tirpitz. No doubt Tirpitz would have been honoured to discover a sow bearing his name.

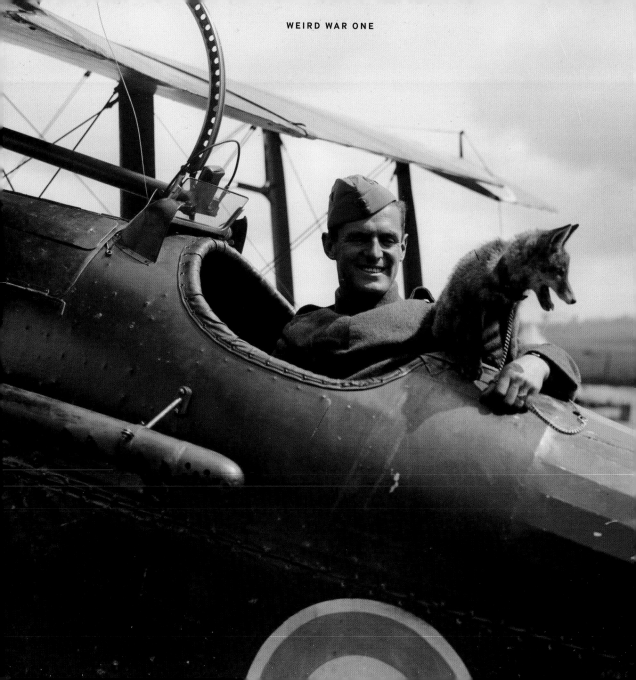

The fox cub mascot

of No. 32 Squadron on the fuselage of a Royal Aircraft
Factory SE5a fighter, Humieres aerodrome, May 1918.
Bravery and audacity were essential attributes for flyers of
all nationalities in their daily brushes with danger and death.
In this image the brush is a soft one and safely attached to
the body of an unusual but friendly pet.

A **German soldier** emerges
from a toilet having lost his
trousers but gained a cat.
One of many wonderful and
strange animal encounters
recorded by off-duty troops.

A Sergeant-Major R.F.A. showing his mascot, a **hedgehog**, to a French girl at Rollencourt Chateau, August 1917. Perhaps he had read and loved Beatrix Potter's books. But the lack of enthusiasm in this young lady suggests that the creature's reputation as a haven for parasites overrode any desire to pet Mrs Tiggy-Winkle.

An Australian corporal offers a **joey** a snack. On board a ship. A very long way from the Bush. Preventing her from jumping overboard must have been a challenge. It is hoped they did not resort to the strategy of 'tie me kangaroo down, sport'.

Snapped at sea: a baby **crocodile** gives a terrier a thing or two to think about. An officer aboard the battlecruiser HMAS *Australia* sports with two of the ship's pets.

Hunting mice and rats at sea is an exhausting business, so while her masters toil, this **cat** rests in her custom-made hammock on the Royal Navy's battlecruiser, HMS *Repulse*.

Home Fronts

FROM MI5 GIRL GUIDES
TO TICKLING STICKS

PAGE 126
Girl Guides did their
bit too. MI5 even
recruited Girl Guides
as messengers at its
London headquarters
during the war. They
originally used Boy
Scouts, but found them
to be too boisterous.
The Guides' 'methods
of getting into mischief
were on the whole less
distressing'. So a special
MI5 Guides company
was formed, and the girls
paraded across the roof
of Waterloo House every
Monday for inspection.

PAGE 127
In perilous times,
superstition can bring
a little comfort. Civilian
Parisians made these
little **wool doll mascots**
as good luck charms.
They were named
Nénette and Rintintin,
and were occasionally
accompanied by their
baby. In 1918, people
wore them as protection
against the shells of
Big Bertha, the long-
range German gun that
bombarded Paris at
intervals between 23
March and 15 August.

THROUGHOUT HISTORY civilians have suffered – directly and indirectly – the consequences of warfare.

In the First World War, security was the most pressing concern for those at home. Fear of invasion led to various 'spy manias' and civilians young and old standing guard at strategic points – coastlines, railways, telephone exchanges and wireless stations. The fate of loved ones at the front was never far from the mind either, and people did what they could to offer support. Collecting conkers, gathering nettles, preparing food parcels – every little helped.

Contributing to the war effort wasn't optional, though, and nor was it usually as enjoyable as knitting socks. Early on in the war governments recognised that the civilians at home were key to financing and creating all the necessary materials to wage war.

Censorship was introduced. Temperance was encouraged, and theatres and pubs closed early (boo!). Food was rationed. Women joined the workforce in all industries and public services. All civilians were urged to back the war out of their own pockets, from incomes ravaged by increased taxation. The British government even interfered with time itself, introducing British Summer Time in May 1916 to exploit the longer summer days in order to boost industrial and agricultural production.

Day after day, civilians did their best to continue as the war crawled on and reports flooded in of casualties at the front. It's little wonder that when the end eventually came, it was greeted by great outpourings of emotion in all countries – and the joyous and pointless invention of the tickling stick...

The must-have accessory for the 1916 season: a flag. These stylishly uniformed women of the volunteer Signallers' Corps transmitting station are learning **semaphore signalling** at a summer camp at Lannock, Hertfordshire.

▶ The style police? Not quite: the National War Savings Committee. This **1916 poster** was designed to discourage thoughtless spending and encourage people to put money into the war effort instead. Being plain and frumpy was far preferable to being unpatriotic.

TO DRESS EXTRAVAGANTLY IN WAR TIME IS WORSE THAN BAD FORM IT IS UNPATRIOTIC

▲ Have these eager **Sea Scouts** accosted a suspicious fisherman? No, they're merely receiving and recording wreckage brought in by the innocent seafarer. In order to release men for fighting, Scouts were recruited to help out with everything from coast watching to working on the land.

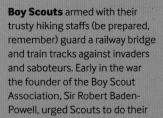

Boy Scouts armed with their trusty hiking staffs (be prepared, remember) guard a railway bridge and train tracks against invaders and saboteurs. Early in the war the founder of the Boy Scout Association, Sir Robert Baden-Powell, urged Scouts to do their bit for the country and join the Scouts: 'Boys of Britain! Don't go about waving flags and shouting because there's a war. Any ass can do that. And don't stay idle doing nothing — that is almost worse. Come and do something for your country.'

An illustration from a young Scout's **letter** to his aunt in February 1916, in which he refers to the Zeppelin danger near Bristol and applauds his aunt's readiness to 'take up a gun and fight the sausage makers'.

51, Berkeley Road
Bishopston
Bristol

FEB. -3 1916

FEB. -3 1916

Dear Auntie Bee,
        I am writing to thank you for your nice Xmas gift.
I think the war is getting worse every day, do you? The Zeps, two days ago, were 23 miles from Bristol, so "look out" or "Be Prepared" is our Scout Motto.
We are all keeping very well, how is Gwen & your self

I am a stamp collector now, I wondered if you had any stamps such as American or Canadian, if so would you send them to me. I have 597 stamps & a nice Album.
The other day we had a huge number (about 60) of Canadian Transports & Canadians on the Downs.
I asked one of the soldiers if they were going to the front, he said "In two days time we shall be in France".
I am glad to hear you are ready to take up a gun & fight the Sausage Makers or Kaiser Billy and Little Willie play with little willie
Good bye for the present,
        With Love Hubert xxxxxx

A Boy Scout bugler sounds the 'all clear' after an air raid.

From the end of October 1917, several hundred Boy Scouts were on regular air raid duty, armed with their trusty bugles.

Boy Scouts, bugles at their sides and bikes at the ready,

receive instructions from an officer at their local police station about sounding the 'all clear' alert (put bugle to lips and blow).

POLICE NOTICE

ALL CLEAR

▲ Some **British air raid warnings** in the First World War were rather more primitive than in the Second. Rather than sounding a siren to say a raid was imminent, policemen would head out by bike with a warning sign slung around their necks. At the end of the raid they'd swap signs and make another circuit.

The often cold and unsanitary conditions of trench warfare meant that all soldiers eventually became 'lousy'. No, not bad at their jobs, but infested with lice. Once inventors back home got wind of this itchy issue, they developed a variety of solutions, each as useless as the last. Most servicemen resorted to 'chatting': destroying lice and eggs in their clothing with a lighted cigarette end or match flame. At least men wearing the **Trenchman** may have felt a little warmer around the middle — or like they were wearing a maternity support belt.

▲ No cotton available? Try nettles instead. This **poster** encourages children to collect nettles to be made into army clothes. Forty kilograms provided enough nettle fibre for one shirt. In 1915, 1.3 million kilograms of nettles were collected in Germany, and the next year they gathered 2.7 million kilograms. That's an awful lot of stinging skin rashes.

A **paper undergarment** from Germany, where cloth shortages were extremely pressing by the end of the war. The wearer must have rustled as she walked. All sorts of unlikely materials including wood as well as paper were employed in the place of cotton for all sorts of garments (including grave shrouds).

An Australian take on the sock shortage. In addition to (enormous) socks, the **Citizens' War Chest Fund**, formed in Sydney two weeks after the war's outbreak, sought to supply all manner of comforts for Australian forces serving in the Middle East, Gallipoli, and on the Western Front.

THE "WAR CHEST" WANTS 150,000 PAIRS SOCKS BEFORE THE END OF JUNE. HELP AT ONCE.

Send to the "WAR CHEST" DEPÔT, 68 Elizabeth St. Sydney.

A special **tape measure for knitting socks**. Early in the war women in the UK and British Empire were encouraged to 'do their bit' by knitting much-needed socks for the troops. The British Secretary of State for War, Lord Kitchener, even took a break from saving the country to contribute a sock pattern featuring a new technique for a seamless join of the toe, still known as the Kitchener stitch.

WEIRD WAR FACT

In the autumn of 1917, Britain was suffering a shortage of cordite, a vital component for munitions. So some enterprising manufacturers began experimenting with extracting acetone, the chemical needed to make cordite, from that beloved schoolyard treasure: the humble conker. Vast quantities of conkers were collected, mostly by schoolchildren, and sent to top-secret factories. But the quality of the conker-derived acetone was poor and the project was halted. Bad for bomb-making, wonderful for childhood innocence.

▶ Hang on, did the Germans share jolly posters forewarning of their Zeppelin attacks? No, this perplexing **poster** was produced in Australia, thousands of miles away from the Zeppelin menace. It relates to an Australian recruiting campaign called the March to Freedom that took place in rural New South Wales in 1918.

◀ A **tickling stick** sold in Trafalgar Square on Armistice Day, 1918. The news of the Armistice in London resulted in scenes of wild exultation. The chimes of the long-silent Big Ben joined the singing, cheering and shrieking of crowds and the bangs of exploding fireworks. The tickling stick was perhaps aimed at those initially resistant to displays of clamouring hysteria; its precise mode of operation is not fully understood.

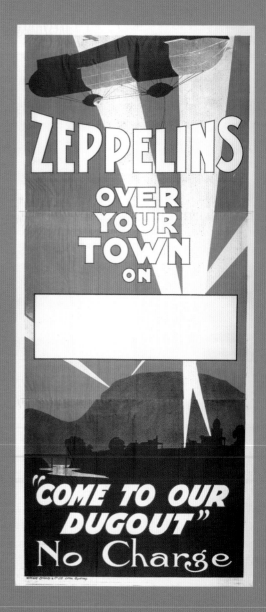

ZEPPELINS OVER YOUR TOWN ON

"COME TO OUR DUGOUT" No Charge

Even 100 or so years ago, the public loved to ooh and ah over dicey stunts. The '**Human Squirrel**' engaged in daring climbing to raise money for war relief funds in New York City. He's shown here at a dizzy height in Times Square in 1918.

Who Says We Ain't Ready

Propaganda

FROM LIBERTY MEASLES
TO KING KONG

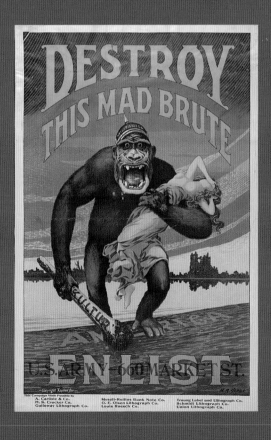

PAGE 138
Every now and again, it's great to throw an inspirational **poster** into the propaganda. Here's one published in the United States in 1917. Nice and uplifting for the country.

PAGE 139
Look familiar? This 1917 US Army **recruiting poster** was surely an inspiration for the popular movie *King Kong* of 1933. It follows a golden rule of propaganda: if you want to destroy your enemy, demonise him first. Oh, and don't bother with subtlety. So this early Kong, wearing a German pickelhaube marked 'militarism' and with a kaiser-like moustache, warns of an enemy who'll ravage the innocent.

PROPAGANDA WAS ESSENTIAL for the war effort to unite populations. Powerful messages were put out to stir up fear and hatred, presenting the enemy as unjust, brutal and inhuman. Men were encouraged, ordered and guilt-tripped into enlisting. Those remaining at home were instructed on how to do their duties, and reminded that their leaders were the bees' knees.

Huge numbers of posters were distributed, newspapers and journals were full of compelling articles, and specially commissioned pamphlets were circulated. Official war artists, correspondents, photographers and cinematographers were granted access to the battle fronts, and relayed inspiring images of the fighting. In the cinemas, battle documentaries and dedicated propaganda cartoons played to large audiences.

Other propaganda was aimed at justifying wartime actions and appeasing neutral countries. But it also attempted to demonise the enemy. Britain shouted of the Germans' 'barbarism' in their use of poison gas, air raids on civilian targets and indiscriminate sinking of neutral shipping. Germany painted the picture of an arrogant Britain breaking international conventions with the naval blockade designed to starve Germany.

When the Americans entered the war in April 1917 on the Allied side, it was because they were sick of unrestricted German submarine warfare. But without doubt, the anti-German messages of the Allied propaganda machine had made their decision easier. Effective propaganda did not determine events, but it did influence them. Sticks and stones could break your bones, and words could either help or hurt you.

TO ARMS!

Samples of

PURE GRIT

Are to be met in abundance in all Training Camps.

GAME COCKS

Cleaning their Spurs.

BIRDS OF THE FEATHER

Welcomed by Fellow-Sports.

NIP INTO THE RING, COBBER,

.. and ..

WIN FAME!

"STIFFEN THE SINEWS, SUMMON UP THE BLOOD!"

ADVERTISER PRINT. ADELAIDE. (Sgd.) J. NEWLAND, Chairman State Recruiting Committee, 4th Military District.

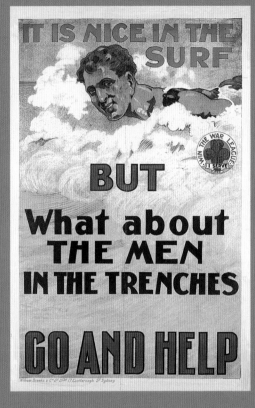

IT IS NICE IN THE SURF

THE WAR LEAGUE
I SERVE

BUT

What about THE MEN IN THE TRENCHES

GO AND HELP

William Brooks & Co Ltd 17 Castlereagh St Sydney

Aussie **recruiting poster** appealing to sports lovers and those of a macho disposition. Why bother illustrating when you can shout with BIG LETTERS compelling words like 'arms', 'grit', 'fame' and 'blood'?

Poster issued by the women-led Win the War League in Australia in an attempt to get men out of swim shorts and into khaki. Members of the League signed a pledge to do all in their power to win the war.

THIS is the FLOWER of the Army, which has been assiduously cultivated in Germany during the past forty ... and has spread over that ... y to the detriment of other ... useful plants. There is ... ently now an approach-... tage of wheat and flour.

... rescence is interesting ... ng one of the most ... c developments of ... he SPIKE.

II.
...ET PLANT
... PRUSSIANUS

III.
THE HELMET PLANT
MILITARISMUS PRUSSIANUS

WAR PLANTS
or
Products of Intensive Kultur.

PREHENSILE SON-FLOWER.
KRONPRINZIA PREHENSILIS.

This plant possesses prehensile vegetative organs which instantly close on anything of value to the plant with which they may come in contact.

Note, too, its very LOFTY STALK. The plant prefers a different habitat from that affected by the Williamia described elsewhere, in fact, the two plants are rarely found in the same district.

LONDON
GEORGE ROUTLEDGE & SONS, LTD.
NEW YORK: E. P. DUTTON & CO.

Not, in fact, a guide to wartime flora and fauna, but a **mock guide** parodying the German military as different species of flowers — including the 'Helmet Plant'.

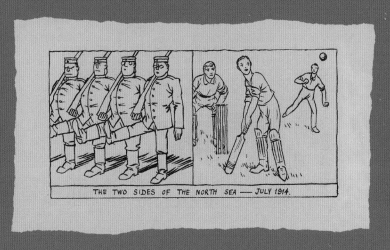

THE TWO SIDES OF THE NORTH SEA — JULY 1914.

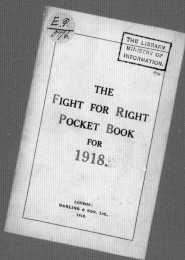

THE
FIGHT FOR RIGHT
POCKET BOOK
FOR
1918.

LONDON:
DARLING & SON, Ltd.,
1918.

The British propaganda *Fight for Right Pocket Book* of 1918 provides a simple explanation of how the war started: the Germans, obsessed with militarism, launch a war of imperial expansion, while the British, innocently occupied with cricket, are mere victims in the path of the Teutonic masses. Not quite!

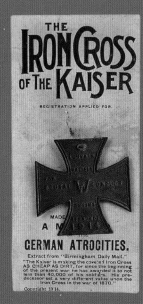

Crosses like this one, sometimes called **sardonic iron crosses**, were commercially produced for British propaganda. They mimicked the German Iron Cross awarded for valour in combat, but were for 'war atrocities' perpetrated by German forces. Just in case you didn't get the message, the cross is embossed with the text 'For Brutal Conduct'. Quite what you were meant to do with such a faux medal, other than wave it about in the pub after a few pints, is unclear.

A **1914 map of Europe** depicting the early stages of the war as a dog fight. Britain is a bulldog held on leash by a British sailor; France, a poodle; Germany, a dachshund; and Austria-Hungary, a mongrel. The bulldog bites the dachshund on the nose. Meanwhile, Serbia is represented by a wasp, and Russia by a bear. This poster was produced in Britain and reproduced in Germany as an example of British propaganda.

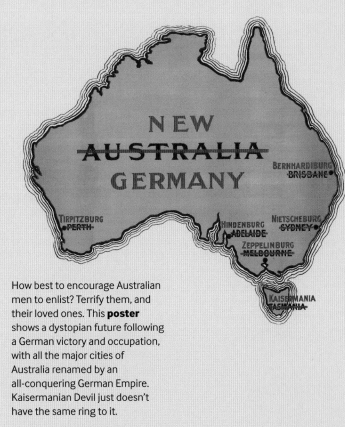

How best to encourage Australian men to enlist? Terrify them, and their loved ones. This **poster** shows a dystopian future following a German victory and occupation, with all the major cities of Australia renamed by an all-conquering German Empire. Kaisermanian Devil just doesn't have the same ring to it.

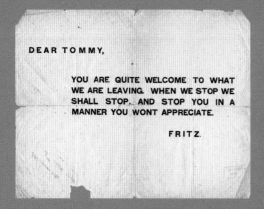

DEAR TOMMY,

YOU ARE QUITE WELCOME TO WHAT WE ARE LEAVING. WHEN WE STOP WE SHALL STOP. AND STOP YOU IN A MANNER YOU WONT APPRECIATE.

FRITZ.

Poet Ernst Lissauer came up with the lovely catchphrase *Gott Strafe England* (God Punish England), which became something of a craze in Germany. In the years before bumper stickers, any object had the potential to bear a slogan, from **teacups** to coal briquettes.

An early example of **propaganda**, dropped by the retreating German forces. On the back of this typescript leaflet is the handwritten note 'Steenwerk, 3 September 1918'. The remorseless Allied advance prompted desperate measures from the retreating German forces (and, apparently, fairly incomprehensible threats).

WEIRD WAR FACT

*In America the government supported a renaming campaign to make things with German names more patriotic. The watchword was **'liberty'**. So frankfurters became **'liberty sausages'**, sauerkraut became **'liberty cabbage'** and dachshunds were **'liberty dogs'**. Most bizarrely of all, you didn't contract German measles, but **'liberty measles'**.*

The British royal family did their own bit of patriotic name-swapping, changing their surname from Saxe-Coburg and Gotha to Windsor by proclamation in 1917.

A **French** marketer's dream: **toilet paper** especially for the anti-Prussians, which 'all good French people and Allies should use'. The title is a pun: 'A Q' sounds like the French *à cul*, meaning 'arse paper'.

Wiping out and flushing the enemy... **British toilet paper** featuring the kaiser's portrait. The German chancellor, von Bethmann-Hollweg, had dismissed the treaty signed by Britain, Prussia and Austria to defend Belgium as a mere 'scrap of paper' after the kaiser's armies invaded the country and Britain declared war in 1914.

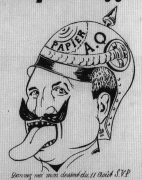

Article bien Français !

PAPIER A. Q.

(Déposé)

Antipruscophile et hygiénique

Donnez moi mon dessert du 11 Août S.V.P.

Tous bons Français et Alliés doivent l'employer

En VENTE partout - La pochette : **0.10**

VENTE EN GROS : 31, Rue Saint-Roch, 31

'More fun than women' and 'easier than chess' — compelling reasons to play the **game** of *QuatrArmes*. The assured and reassuring presence of French Commander Joseph Joffre ('Papa' Joffre) looks pretty confident, but Crown Prince Friedrich Wilhelm ('Little Willie') is having to think hard. No prizes for guessing who's going to win the game.

JEU DES QUATRARMES BREVETÉ. S.G.D.G.

PLUS AMUSANT QUE LES DAMES   PLUS SIMPLE QUE LES ÉCHECS

▼ Who knew **skittles** could be so patriotic? Players could *strike* down the enemy with this set in which each skittle represents a different leader.

Beat back the HUN with LIBERTY BONDS

F. Strothmann.

ARE YOU FOND OF CYCLING?

IF SO

WHY NOT CYCLE FOR THE KING?

RECRUITS WANTED

By the S. Midland Divisional Cyclist Company

(Must be 19, and willing to serve abroad).

CYCLES PROVIDED. Uniform and Clothing issued on enlistment.

Application in person or by letter to Cyclists, The Barracks, Gloucester.

BAD TEETH NO BAR.

H. Osborne, Printer, St. Mary's Square, Gloucester.

Cycling was massively popular in Britain in 1914, and it was only fitting that the Army should exploit this obsession with this **recruitment poster**. The fact that they were willing to accept cyclists with poor teeth speaks volumes about the pressing need for men. Army dentists and 'mechanics' had their work cut out getting the new recruits in as good physical order as their army-issue bikes!

More demonising imagery of the enemy in this **poster** exploiting the word 'Hun', three letters designed to convey ruthlessness and barbarism. Possibly the Germans weren't too bothered by the association; after all, in 1900 Kaiser Wilhelm had encouraged his troops setting off for China to be like the legendarily bloodthirsty Huns of Attila.

WEIRD WAR FACT

*Britain had suffered badly from negative propaganda in relation to its treatment
of enemy civilians during the second Anglo-Boer War (1899–1902).
So right after the First World War broke out, the Brits were on the case.
The War Propaganda Bureau was formed in August 1914, and it deployed the
best and most respected writers of the day – including H G Wells, John Masefield
and Sir Arthur Conan Doyle – to be powerful, persuasive PRs.
They wrote books and articles for the home front, the USA and
other neutrals and allies, to rally support for the war.*

◀ An attempt to guilt-trip dog lovers into enlisting. Because of course this **Red Cross war dog** is a stirring example of selfless commitment, having knowingly and intelligently enlisted for duty.

▶ A spitfire of a hell cat sums up the violent potential of the **US Tank Corps** in a war to the finish. Helpfully, the poster artist clarifies that it's men, and not cats, who are enlisting.

This **recruiting poster** for the US Navy is a lusty celebration of energy, innocence and enthusiasm. The image of the American sailor astride the speeding homing torpedo calls to mind the launching of the US nuclear weapon from a B-52 in Stanley Kubrick's 1964 black comedy *Dr Strangelove*.

▶ A British Army **recruiting poster** of 1914 trying to exact some moral pressure with a spot of good old-fashioned politeness.

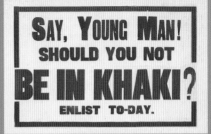

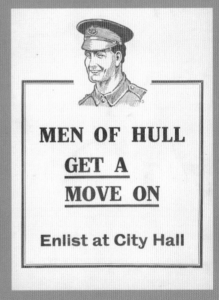

Dispense with politeness – give it to them straight! Posters focusing on a particular town or city were used by the British Army to get groups of men to enlist together in so-called Pals battalions. This **poster** may relate to the formation of the 10th (Service) Battalion, East Yorkshire Regiment, known as the 1st Hull or Hull Commercials.

▶ Recent **recruits** wait for their pay in the churchyard of St. Martin in the Fields, Trafalgar Square, London, August 1914.

MEN OF MILLWALL

Hundreds of Football enthusiasts are joining the Army daily.

Don't be left behind.

Let the Enemy hear the "LION'S ROAR."

Join and be in at

THE FINAL

and give them a

KICK OFF THE EARTH

Apply:
West Africa House, opposite National Theatre, Kingsway.

Association Football was as popular in 1914 as it is today (though match tickets were considerably cheaper then!). This British **recruiting poster** urges supporters of Millwall FC (nicknamed The Lions) to join up and fight the enemy. Those who did enlist may have found themselves chasing a football into no man's land: they were booted out to encourage infantry advances at the Battle of Loos (September 1915) and on the first day of the Battle of the Somme (1 July 1916).

Food and Drink

FROM A PICKLED MONKEY TO
A SCURVY TRICK

THE ARMIES AND NAVIES of the opposing nations in the First World War were unprecedented in size, and feeding them required herculean efforts of organisation, supply and distribution. Some nations fared better than others. The low morale in the Imperial Russian armies in late 1916 had a lot to do with the fact that they were ravenous. In contrast, British servicemen had at least one hot meal a day. Still, theirs was a pretty boring diet and far from gourmet; the biscuits, in particular, were liable to break teeth. Thank goodness for food parcels from home and, for troops in France and Belgium, the odd feast of egg and chips in a local café.

Hungry soldiers staved off their hunger pangs with tobacco. As for a tipple, the British authorities frowned on soldiers under the influence, but occasionally allowed a ration of rum, especially before 'going over the top'. The French, though, wouldn't dream of asking men to do their jobs without a *pinard*, a daily allowance of wine.

While the men on the front may have dreamed of delicious, filling Sunday lunches cooked up by their mums back home, the truth was those mums were no longer laying on hearty spreads. In this first 'total war', both sides sought to starve the other to death through naval blockades and attacks on supply ships. The result was serious food shortages, and snaking queues outside shops became a common sight.

Soon governments introduced coupon-based ration schemes, and launched educational campaigns. Economising, being creative in the kitchen and growing your own food were the calls to duty for civilians. Little did they know that they were sowing the seeds for the famous 'Waste Not, Want Not' and 'Dig for Victory' schemes of another great war, coming all too soon.

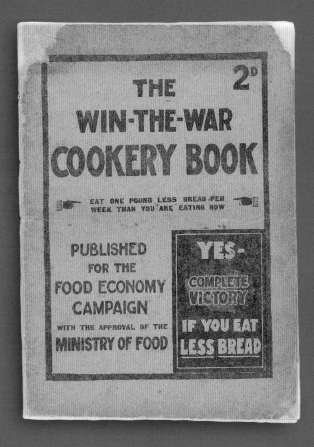

Such a dramatic call to action in this **poster,** but in fact the result was women grappling not with the underwater menace but with the contents of their pantries. Flour and wheat imports were particularly hard hit by Germany's attempt to blockade Britain using U-boats. So it became the patriotic duty of housewives to make food stocks go a long way.

How could a hungry Brit manage on less bread? The key, according to this **cookbook,** was to make each mouthful last much longer by chewing, and chewing, and chewing. An added bonus (besides 'complete victory' in the war) was a longer life. Apparently, poorly chewed food leads to 'stomach struggle', which is ultimately fatal. As this book memorably puts it: 'Probably seven people out of ten are digging their graves with their teeth, and they never tire of the job.' Such a delightful mental image.

'Your King and Country Need You
and This Is How They Feed You'

– so read graffiti by a disgruntled soldier. **Army biscuits** were the worst. They were so hard that the solider faced a choice: 1) break teeth attempting to consume; 2) soak in hot water to make a vile but edible sludgy mess; 3) find another use, such as firelighter or... photo frame? Sergeant M Herring made this frame from his biscuit to display a picture of him with his wife and twins.

Rouen Base Supply Depot, January 1917. No, the Army Service Corps weren't building a pyramid – these are rations to be dispatched by train to the front.

There is nothing to put in the place of

BEER

a necessity to the

Strength of Britain

"We've won on Beer before; We'll win with Beer again."

This **Bier stein** was donated by the family of Bill Tucker, who served in the Army Ordnance Corps. The inscription is dedicated to the German Husaren-Regiment König Wilhelm I.

A **British beer bottle** from the First World War period, found on the Western Front in the autumn of 1976. Beer wasn't officially allowed in the British front line, but bottles were smuggled in. Officers were allowed a drink, however – often whisky.

The brewers fight back. An **advertisement** from the Brewers' Society explains the importance of beer to the war effort for the strength it creates (no mention of the four-pint jelly legs).

◀ First World War period **British Army rum jar**. The letters SRD stand for Supply Reserve Depot (though soldiers would joke they meant Seldom Reaches Destination, Service Rum Diluted or Soon Runs Dry). Soldiers on active service could be issued with an eighth of a pint of rum at the discretion of their commander or on the recommendation of their medical officer, usually during or after the dawn stand-to and sometimes before going into action.

'Rum jar' was also the British soldiers' nickname for a German trench mortar bomb that was similar in shape. Best to clarify which kind of rum jar is coming your way before reaching for it, then.

'PIONEER' POSTERS, No. 15.

"WE ARE FIGHTING GERMANY, AUSTRIA, AND DRINK; AND, AS FAR AS I CAN SEE, THE GREATEST OF THESE THREE DEADLY FOES IS DRINK."

THE RIGHT HON. D. LLOYD GEORGE.

March 29th, 1915.

Issued by the Temperance Department of the Wesleyan Methodist Church, Tuthill Street, Westminster, S.W.

Don't Take Alcoholic Drinks on MONDAYS.

In view of the great sacrifices freely made by our sailors and soldiers, the National Organizing Committee feels sure that all who remain at home will willingly help the Country in this way.

PRINTED BY ROBERTS & LEETE LTD, LONDON.

Future Prime Minister Lloyd George had a bee in his bonnet about **temperance** – or, failing that, moderation. Hungover workers did nothing to boost industrial output. What to do? First, cut down pub serving hours and ban drinkers from buying rounds. Then, announce that the king has pledged to be teetotal for the course of the war. The king was fairly peeved at this development, and later claimed he'd been forced into it by a 'scurvy trick'.

The **anti-alcohol poster campaign** had its work cut out. Lloyd George may have been a model of sobriety, but Prime Minister Herbert Asquith's liking for the strong stuff was well-known and even celebrated in a song from the popular hit 1916 show, 'The Big Boys are Here'.

WEIRD WAR FACT

Although famous for their love of sausages, the Germans were forced to ban their manufacture for a while during the war. They needed the cow intestines they used as skins for sausages (delicious!) to make the bags that held the gas inside each Zeppelin. A single airship required the guts of more than 250,000 cows. One more reason you wouldn't want to be beneath an exploding Zeppelin.

◄ Having the 'wurst' of times… German troops sharing a meal in the **sausage store** in their quarters. Presumably their pet dog has had its sausage ration for the day.

Two German soldiers show off a **giant beetroot** they've grown near Martincourt, 1917. The British also applied green fingers to trench gardens, growing root and salad vegetables. Civilians helped out too: Messrs. Sutton and Sons planted 4,000 cabbages in transport lines at Rabot.

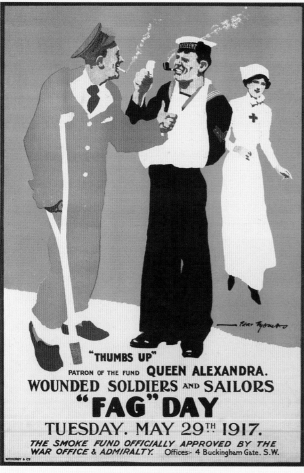

Thumbs up to **'Fag' Day**... Just about everyone smoked cigarettes ('gaspers' to officers and 'fags' to soldiers), and in 1916 tobacco was included in British rations for the first time. The health concerns were not widely known and were outweighed by the comfort the soldiers took in smoking. Special charities were set up to ensure troops received cigarettes, tobacco and pipes.

Back home, rationing didn't kick in until 1918, but U-boats sinking supply ships meant shortages started earlier. So, how best to warn British people off gluttony? Why the **Wartime Bread and Butter Plate** of course! It featured a message from the prime minister reminding the diner not to each too much.

Vin blonk makes me zigzag...

'I went up the Aunt Sally and got some barker and pomfritz, but I missed mopping up some jippo with my Japan, so I ended up with canteen medals...'

Are you lost?

Don't worry – here's a crash course in soldier food slang:

Aunt Sally – ration truck (from a nickname for the Army Service Corps)
Baby's head – meat suet pudding
Barker – sausage (from an old song about a Dutchman's dog)
Burgoo – porridge
Canteen medals – beer or food stains down the front of the uniform
(more usually beer)
Dog and maggot – biscuit and cheese
Duff – suet pudding
Japan – bread (from the French *du pain*)
Jippo – bacon gravy or juice
Pickled monkey – a mystery meat fed to POWs by the Germans
Pomfritz – chips
Shackles – stew made from leftovers
Spotted dog – currant suet
Vin blonk – white wine
Wad – sandwich
Zigzag – drunk

WEIRD WAR FACT

Sugar was heavily restricted, and ice cream was one of the casualties. Bamboozled ice cream manufacturers were forced to get creative in freezing sugar-free mixtures. One day — ta da! They invented that sticky, headache-inducing but wonderfully refreshing treat, the ice lolly.

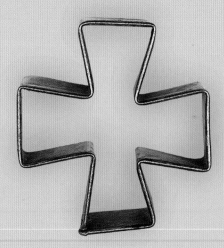

In July 1917 this **inkpot** went on sale, designed to serve as a daily reminder to save... no, not squashed mushrooms, but bread. In May of that year some master baker had realised Britain had only six weeks of flour left, and the 'Save Bread' campaign was launched.

The Germans were having their own problems with food supplies in the later part of the war, which meant substitute ingredients aplenty. How do you make a bland biscuit taste better? Cut it out with this patriotic **pastry-cutter** in the shape of the Iron Cross, a German military decoration.

EAT MORE COTTAGE CHEESE

ONE POUND SUPPLIES MORE PROTEIN THAN

One pound of beef, or

One pound of pork, or

One pound of lamb, or

One pound of veal, or

One pound of fowl

YOU'LL NEED LESS MEAT

A Postal Card Will Bring Recipes

for using this meat substitute

U. S. DEPARTMENT OF AGRICULTURE, WASHINGTON, D. C.

COTTAGE CHEESE OR MEAT **?** ASK YOUR POCKETBOOK **!**

Across the ocean, Americans were urged to save meat and wheat to supply to Britain. The answer, according to this **poster**: nosh down on platefuls of cottage cheese.

Time Out

FROM DRAMA IN DRAG TO
EGG-AND-SPOON CAMEL RACES

Souvenir Program

OF

Imperial Camel Brigade

SPORTS

Somewhere in Palestine

12th - 13th February 1918.

PAGE 168
The **'Queerios' concert party** at the British Army General Headquarters (GHQ) in Montreuil-sur-Mer, 1918. The transformation from male to female could be very convincing, as reported by Lieutenant G Havard Thomas in January 1918 after seeing the pantomime *Dick Whittington*: 'The boy who took the part of the girl acted so well that it was difficult to believe it was actually a man.'

PAGE 169
Among the sports played by this camel-mounted infantry brigade was a **'camel race'**. But not just any old camel race – an egg-and-spoon camel race. Spirit-raising hilarity for those serving abroad. Well, if they could find the race 'somewhere in Palestine'.

THE FIRST WORLD WAR was the first 'total' war: it massively affected the lives of many millions of service personnel as well as civilians on the home fronts. People were under constant stress, and they needed distractions.

For those at home, there was a wide choice of public houses, theatres, concert halls and music halls, together with the well-established and very popular cinemas. Or, if you fancied a night in, you could play 'Waiting for the Willies': one of the patriotic board games designed to entertain and keep up the fighting spirit.

At the front, there was little opportunity for the soldier to engage in recreational activities, though in very quiet sectors trench art souvenir making, covert gambling and even gardening were attempted. The strong appeal of popular music also meant that some of the better-equipped dugouts boasted gramophones.

Beyond the range of the guns, nothing beat 'a spot o' culture' for escapism, for inspiration and, when it came to male actors in drag, for a good laugh. Concert parties carried on the tradition of the music hall, and 'smoking parties' offered a chance to drift on the melodies of soloists and pianists. Regular theatrical productions were staged behind the lines (and even in prisoner of war camps, despite the scant resources available).

But for many men then (as now), sport was king. Football dominated, and officers regularly took part as a means of bonding with their men. Lots of officers favoured riding as a leisure activity; some even organised competitive divisional horse shows. For the more sedentary, fishing was a popular option. And for the more combative, there was always... mop fighting?

The show must go on, despite the **Zeppelin raids** over London. After the first Zeppelin raid on the capital in May 1915 resulted in serious damage to Theatreland, audiences for shows were disappointingly small. So theatres able to provide reliable protection took every opportunity to advertise their Zepp-proof features.

The **Vaudeville Theatre** in London's Strand makes clear its intention to keep calm and carry on despite hostile air raids. After a Zeppelin raid in October 1915 on the Strand and Aldwych, the Vaudeville (together with the other theatres in the vicinity) was used as an emergency first aid post.

The bizarrely named **National Doll League Children's Unconscious Doll Exerciser:** a doll with springs for arms. It was patented by professional strongman and fitness expert Eugene Sandow in 1915 and marketed by the National Doll Organisation. Modelled on a First World War soldier, this doll was aimed at boys (dolls in nurses' uniforms were made for girls). The idea was that children 'unconsciously' exercise through play, and each doll came with details of 21 games to get kids moving. A noble aim, certainly.

'**Waiting for the Willies**': an example of commercial games manufacturers seizing on the spirit of the times. The two 'Willies' are the German kaiser and the crown prince, and your mission is to consign them to imprisonment on 'St Helena' and put Europe back to rights by restoring the flags to their respective corners.

The idea of this hand-held **Trench Football** game is to dribble (roll) a ball-bearing to the goal: the kaiser's mouth. But look out for the traps along the way, marked with caricatures of German military leaders. The game is helpfully marked 'British Design, British Made', just in case there was any doubt.

Here's a cheery **game** for all
the family: 'War Tactics, or
Can Great Britain Be Invaded?'
In the run-up to the war British
people were fixated on the
invasion threat. For example,
Guy du Maurier's 1909 play
An Englishman's Home was
an instant theatrical hit. It
swelled the ranks of the
newly formed Territorial
Force, whose original primary
function was home defence.

Douglas, a **dummy** used by Arthur Langley Handen in his ventriloquist act to entertain the troops. Handen was attached to a colonel's staff in the Royal Artillery and he stated, 'I reckon that doll saved my life – the colonel enjoyed him so much that he prevented my posting elsewhere and mildly discouraged me from taking the offer of going for a commission.' So saying, the shrapnel hole in the dummy's case suggests that his owner was never far from danger.

'We'll never live this down...'

Two German prisoners of war in clown costumes ready for a theatrical show at 360 POW Company, France. Prisoners on both sides loved these shows. The performers had to rely on limited resources for costumes and scenery – in this case, the costumes are made from sacking.

A **dress rehearsal for _Cinderella,_** performed by the Royal Flying Corps Kite and Balloon section in France, 1918. The fairy godmother is evidently delighted to be playing his part.

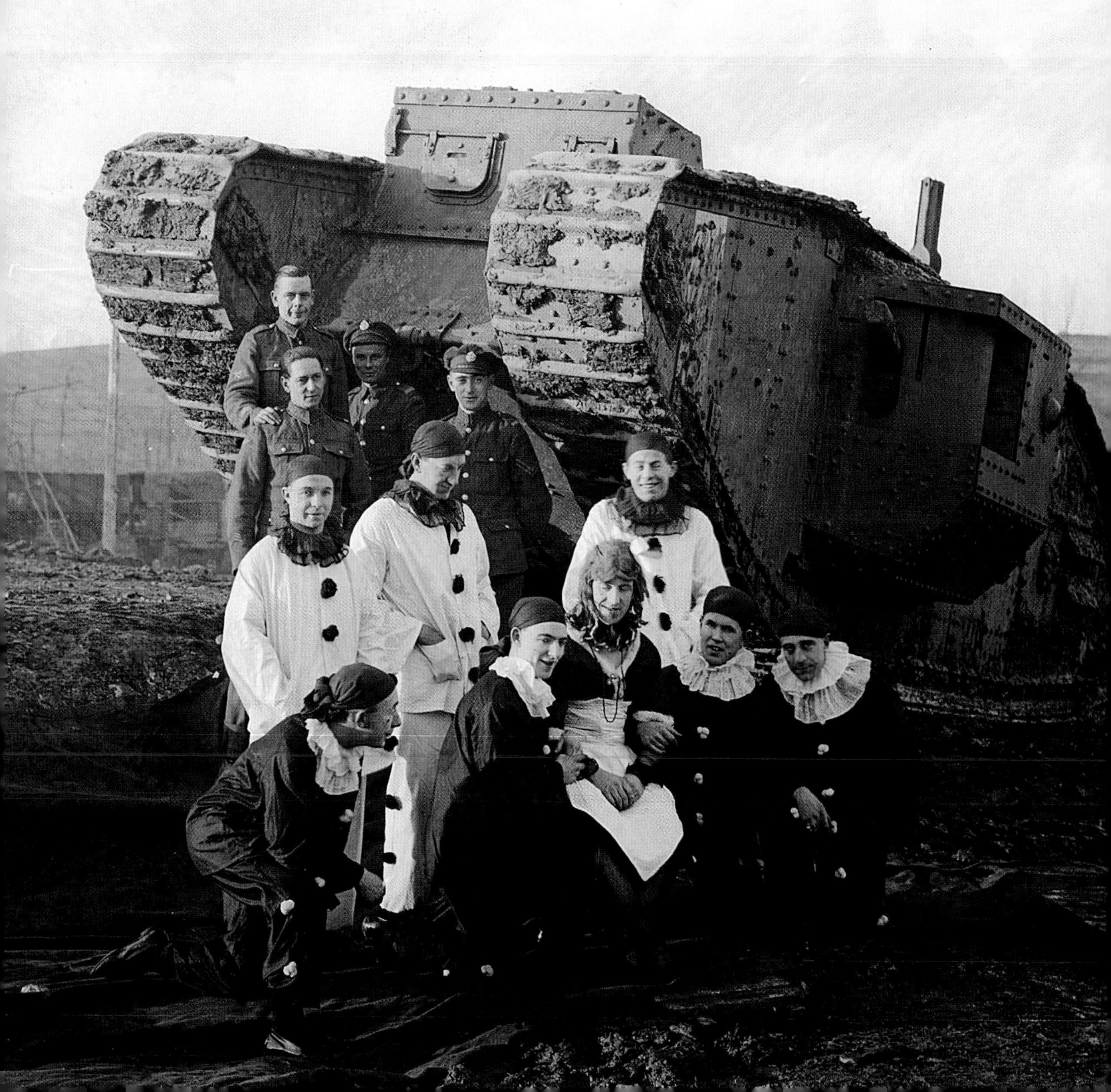

◀ The **Concert Party** at Central Stores, Tank Corps. Clown (or *pierrot*) costumes were a popular choice for entertainments at the time.

Men of war assume any necessary disguise: in this case, **Royal Navy officers** on board the battleship HMS *Royal Oak* are making up to put on a show, *The Scarlet Pimpernel* The leading 'lady' is game now, but wait until she tries walking in that trailing skirt.

An actor of **Maple Leaves,** the Canadian Concert Party, putting on his lippy in a field on the Western Front, 1917. With women rarely permitted close to the front line, most concert parties had an actor who specialised in female roles. With demurely crossed ankles, this actor's getting into character before he even dons his wig.

Où irons-nous ce soir ??

Voir ces Dames

chez Madame JULIETTE

7, Rue Héronval, ARRAS

ENGLISH SPOKEN   8327

A rather racy **publicity flyer** for night-life entertainment in Arras. It reads,

'Where are we going tonight??

To see these girls.'

Chez Madame Juliette thoughtfully employed English-speaking hostesses to meet the 'needs' of British servicemen.

Dancing was popular with the troops, but the scarcity of women at the front was an obstacle. The solution? Take a deep breath, grab the hand of the nearest bloke and dance with each other. Here Allied troops, watched by slouch-hatted Anzacs, dance to music from a French marine band in Salonika.

The cavalry demonstrate their sword skills at Lambet Camp in Salonika, 1916, in a... **lemon-cutting tournament.** Yes, boredom was an issue on the Salonika front, which was far quieter than the Western Front. One Lieutenant noted in his diary in July 1917: 'Calm still reigns on the front and to relieve the monotony our batteries fire on hay makers and — worse still — bathing parties'.

How to boost morale and keep young men fit and active?

Why, set them to mop fighting, of course. These soldiers are at the Military Sports Day in Felixstowe, September 1916. This still is from a film; keep watching and you see fierce combat and then... victory! A mop-lance takes down one teetering soldier.

Who said the staff had no sense of humour?

Brigadier-General W S Swabey engaging in piggyback antics on the Italian front. A case of life imitating, or at least anticipating, art: the scene calls to mind the memorable song 'They Were Only Playing Leapfrog' in Richard Attenborough's 1969 film *Oh! What a Lovely War*.

Swapping weapon for watering can, a soldier of the Gordon Highlanders (51st Division) tending his **trench garden** in Heninel, October 1917. Vegetables were of most use, but soldiers grew flowers as well. The historian C R M F Cruttwell recalled a trench garden near Ploegsteert in 1915 that boasted a clump of Madonna lilies and a red rose.

 Soldiers **fishing** in the Yser Canal near Boesinghe, January 1918. One is using a rifle as a fishing rod, the other a corkscrew barbed-wire support. Animal rights activists look away now: unsporting soldiers sometimes fished with hand grenades, dropping them into canals or lakes where the ensuing explosions would stun their prey.

Nurses of the Queen Alexandra's Imperial Military Nursing Service Reserve (QAIMNSR) and the Territorial Force Nursing Service (TFNS) taking part in a **fishing contest** on hospital barges, Watten, on the Western Front, June 1918. One lady's lucked out and ended up with a short-poled net.

Wartime **poster** in praise of the Decca gramophone. Aimed at all service personnel, gramophones even found their way to the front. There, they were beloved but argued over: which music to play? Royal Fusilier Officer Christopher Stone wrote in January 1917: 'Of course we all have different tastes, the colonel's running to waltzes and soft gentle things, Adams to baritone songs, the doctor to banjo and ragtime...' Christopher Stone became the first British disc-jockey after the war.

Not quite 'wine, women and song', but nearly:

British officers enjoy a drink and music from a gramophone outside their metal-roofed shelter at Givenchy, January 1918.

Washing done and pegged on the line to dry, tank officers relax at Poperinghe, September 1917.

A game of cards, papers to read, a dog to pet and a gramophone filling the air with cheery music... if only they were home, it would be a top afternoon.

Celebrations
in Trafalgar Square,
London on
Armistice Day
11th November
1918

Picture List

All images © IWM unless otherwise stated. Every effort has been made to contact all copyright holders, the publishers will be glad to make good in future editions any error or omissions brought to their attention.

PAGE 6-7
Introduction

NTB 263-2

PAGE 8-21
Leaders

Q 53537; EPH 8728; Q 65860 © Getty Images; IWM PST 2734; Q 41927; HU 68367; EPH 7316; EPH 847; EPH 5002; EPH 4303; EPH 9359; Q 48464; IWM PST 2734; EPH 706; EPH C Song G. 77; Documents.13978/F; EPH 4083; EPHEM 325; Woodrow Wilson portrait © Getty Images; EPH 7061; EPH 7062; EPH 7060; EPH 7063; EPH 7065; EPH 9427; EPH 8731; EPH 1243

PAGE 22-37
Soldiering On

Image courtesy US National Archives © Artist's Estate; IWM ART 15600 © Artist's Estate; 59527 © Artist's Estate; EPH 9022; 02/867; FEQ 935; Q 53674; IWM PST 13686; EPH 1308; EPH 2024; FEQ 366; FEQ 31; FEQ 37; FEQ 76; FEQ 99; FEQ 28; EPH.C Greetings © Artist's Estate; Q 86990; IWM PST 10981; UNI 978; EQU 3812; EQU 3911; Souvenir portrait, officer festooned with flowers, and tall and short soldier images all courtesy of Drake Goodman © Artist's Estate; EPH 2779; EPH 8262

PAGE 38-53
Camouflage

Q 13392; © The Royal Society of Marine Artists; Image courtesy of the Library of Congress © Artist's Estate; SP 1650; Image courtesy US National Archives, photo no.

530710 © Artist's Estate; UNI 8312; UNI 6060; Q 45738 © J Granville Squiers; SP 1295; MOD 2471; MOD 2474; MOD 2009; MOD 2274; MOD 2037; MOD 2025; Q 27501; MOD 542; AIR 261; Q 17681; Q 95955; Q 17779; Q 17685; E AUS 4938; HU 53370; Q 10310; Q 10308

PAGE 54-67
Inventions and Gadgets

8380 © Artist's Estate; FEQ 1218; IWM PST 2702 © Henri Montassier; Access PROC 767; Access PROC 766; Q 54383; MUN 3206; Q 34135; Q 67038; HU 108117; FIR 11624; FEQ 859; FEQ 492; 3937; Q 24262; Q 45513; Q 31350; Image courtesy Drake Goodman © Artist's Estate; FEQ 886; Q 47886; COM 476; EPH 7354; Image courtesy US National Archives, photo no 533695 © Artist's Estate

PAGE 68-81
Flight

Q 69473; Image courtesy US National Archives © Artist's Estate; Q 23917; IWM PST 2785; EPH 4891; EPH 3471; Q 63768; Q 67559; Q 66807; Q 27476; Q 60465; Q 69930 © Artist's Estate; Q 69929 © Artist's Estate; Image courtesy US National Archives, photo no. 533662 © Artist's Estate; Q 12193; AIR 288

PAGE 82-95
Communication

Q 1152; EPH 2513; Q 27983; Q 18859; Q 1400; Q 79569; AIR 235; Documents.9139; EPH 9028; 76194; Q 30160; MH 34058; K 86/1605; HU 59436; K 86/1605; Documents.7161 © Gail Phillips

Acknowledgements

Many thanks to Philip Dutton and to the staff of Imperial War Museums for their help, in particular Elizabeth Bowers, Madeleine James, Caitlin Flynn, Abigail Lelliott, Steve Woolford, Tony Richards and Terry Charman.
Thanks also to Philip Gilderdale and Carole Ash for their design skill and patience.

The following people kindly supplied material or helped with research:

Martin Bastone, V&A; Roy Behrens, Camoupedia; Glenn Berg; Bob Eckstein; Drake Goodman (Brett Butterworth); Brett Holman, Airminded.org; Dr Hilda Keen; Dr Mike Rogers, Lincolnshire County Council; Dr David Wilson; Chris Woodward (author of The London Palladium: *The Story of The Theatre and its Stars*).